THE TRUTH ABOUT HUMAN TRAFFICKING

THE TRUTH ABOUT HUMAN TRAFFICKING

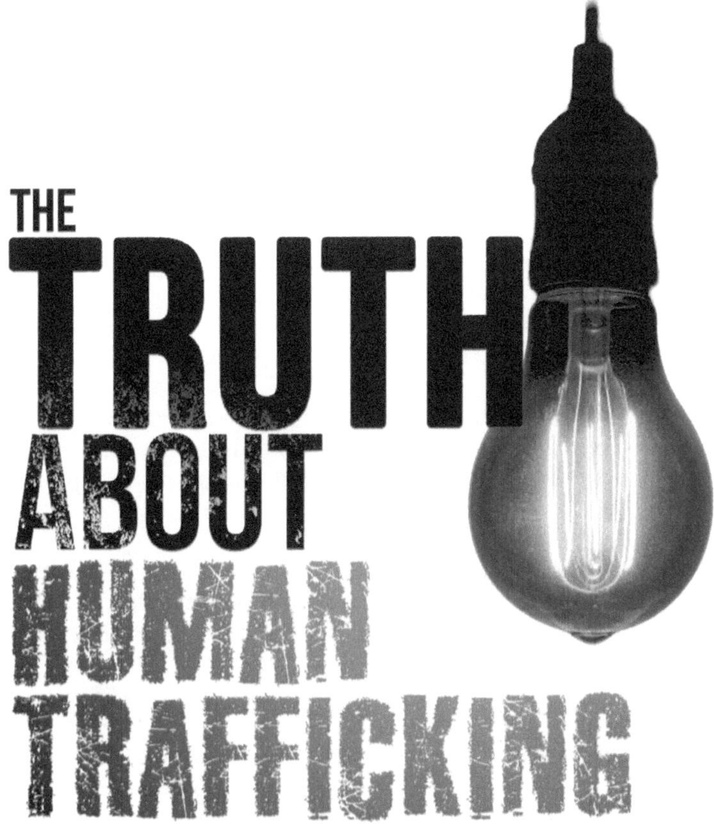

Shining Light on the Realities of Exploitation, the Power of Survival, & the Hope of Restoration

Survivor
SANDY STORM

The Truth About Human Trafficking: Shining Light on the Realities of Exploitation, the Power of Survival, and the Hope of Restoration
Copyright © 2026 by Sandy Storm

Disclaimer
This book is intended for educational and informational purposes only and is based on the author's personal experiences and perspectives. While every effort has been made to ensure accuracy, some names, identifying details, and locations have been altered or changed to protect privacy.

This work contains descriptions of abuse and traumatic events that may be distressing to some readers. The content is not intended to serve as medical, legal, or therapeutic advice, nor should it be used as a substitute for professional guidance.

The author and publisher disclaim any liability for any loss, damage, or disruption arising from the use of this material or from any errors or omissions, whether such errors or omissions result from negligence, accident, or any other cause.

Footprint Publishing
FootprintPub.com

For more information or to contact the author, please email sandy@authorsandystorm.com.

ISBN: 978-1-945786-13-6 (softcover)
ISBN: 978-1-945786-12-9 (hardcover)
ISBN: 978-1-945786-14-3 (eBook)

Cover design and interior by: Amy Harrell Smith, Precision Book Editing
Author photos provided by: Michelle Varley, Varley's Photography
Artwork used by permission.

First printing: January 2026

DEDICATION

For the Family Stalwarts and the Stewarts of Truth...

CONTENTS

CONTENTS

FOREWORD

Truth. It's a word we hear often, but in the world of sex trafficking, it's usually buried under denial, misconceptions, and silence. Truth isn't just about facts—it's about facing the uncomfortable, about pulling back the curtain on what we *think* we know and confronting what's really happening to our most vulnerable.

For nearly 14 years, I worked undercover in Phoenix as a female detective targeting sex trafficking operations. I stood on street corners and in hotel rooms, where I was solicited by thousands of sex buyers and approached by traffickers who tried to recruit, groom, and control me—without knowing I was law enforcement. As an investigator, I lived inside that dark world, saw how it worked from the inside out, and felt the weight of what victims endure. But let me be clear: my experience is not the same as surviving exploitation. I had a way out. Most victims don't. What this book offers is the truth, more than what I witnessed. This book offers a firsthand account and a deep respect for the truth survivors carry—like the one you're about to read—as the mechanics of this crime are explained from the inside out. This book offers a solution to how often the public gets it wrong—not out of malice, but out of ignorance.

That's what makes this book so important.

Sandy Storm, the survivor who wrote this—whose courage you'll see on every page—takes truth and drags it into the light. Her story is more than survival. It's education. It's revelation. It's hope.

One of the most powerful moments in her book is when she realizes, long after the fact, that she *was* a victim of trafficking. For years, she believed the lies—that what happened was somehow her fault. This is one of trafficking's most insidious effects: it convinces victims they chose it. That they deserved it. That no one will believe them. The truth she discovered—that she was manipulated, groomed, and exploited—is the same truth that too many others still haven't been told.

She also exposes another reality people miss: that trafficking isn't always about strangers in the dark. Victims often know and trust their traffickers. These are people who pose as protectors, partners, even friends—until they tighten the leash. Trafficking doesn't always start with violence. It starts with *grooming*—with subtle control, emotional manipulation, isolation, and the slow dismantling of a person's sense of self. By the time the abuse is in full force, the victim is trapped in ways most outsiders can't even begin to see.

Sandy explains with clarity how traffickers create bonds that feel unbreakable. These bonds aren't just emotional—they're psychological, spiritual, and economic. She breaks down the process in a way only someone who's lived it can. And in doing so, she opens the eyes of readers who may have never understood what trafficking really looks like.

Now that I'm retired from law enforcement, my mission continues through my organization, www.achanceforawareness.com. My work is twofold:

- First, I too bring education and awareness to communities through speaking engagements and resources like my book, *Talk to Them*, which helps adults navigate difficult but necessary conversations with youth about online dangers, grooming, and exploitation.
- Second, I train law enforcement—because if we don't equip officers with the right tools and understanding, we'll keep missing victims who are hiding in plain sight.

Sandy offers something I've seen too little of in this field: *real understanding paired with real hope.* She isn't just telling her story. She's calling all of us to think differently, speak up, and act.

This book will challenge you. It will reframe what you thought you knew. It will give you new language, new insight, and new urgency. And if you let it, it will move you toward action—whether that means talking to your kids, questioning your assumptions, supporting survivors, or demanding better from the systems meant to protect the vulnerable.

Let the words you read here stay with you. Let them light the path toward a deeper truth: that ending trafficking starts with seeing it clearly— and that prevention is possible when awareness meets action.

Heidi Chance

Retired Detective
Founder, www.achanceforawareness.com

TRIGGER WARNING

Dear Reader,

While you prepare to take this journey to discover the TRUTH about human trafficking, please prepare your heart to process the information about trafficking you will read in this book. Starting in Chapter 4, I share my story of surviving trafficking, and included in the content are references to child abuse, rape, drug addiction, and other forms of evil. Reading about these events might be triggering for some readers. The stories and examples used are for educational purposes and are not sensationalized or designed to spark emotion; however, it would be impossible not to have an emotional reaction when discussing the wicked ways traffickers exploit their victims.

We want to be wise and aware of the facts, but we don't want to dwell so much on the darkness and sadness that we lose hope. As you read, please protect your heart and be aware of any sensations of fear, anger, or other strong emotions that may come up. You also may have memories or flashbacks of difficult situations you or a loved one has experienced that are similar to the stories in this book. If these issues arise, I encourage you to take the time necessary to process them and take the next steps needed for you to remain healthy and whole.

If you are triggered while reading, please practice self-care and take some time to focus on the goodness in our world. As a trauma survivor, I deal with symptoms of complex PTSD and have sought treatment from mental health and medical professionals for over a decade. Some of my favorite ways I have learned to manage emotional triggers include talking with my husband, Robert, calling or texting a friend, listening to soothing music, engaging in simple breathing and grounding exercises, taking a fifteen- or twenty-minute walk, and playing with or petting my dogs, Cosmo and Kanga. Gratitude and thankfulness are also powerful tools for releasing hope and remaining positive in the face of evil that exists in our world.

You can try any or all of these techniques to practice self-care or seek a specific way to manage triggers. If you experience severe emotional distress and are in the United States, you can call or text 988 to talk or chat with someone anytime, day or night. It's important to care for your soul as you learn the TRUTH about human trafficking and how you can end it.

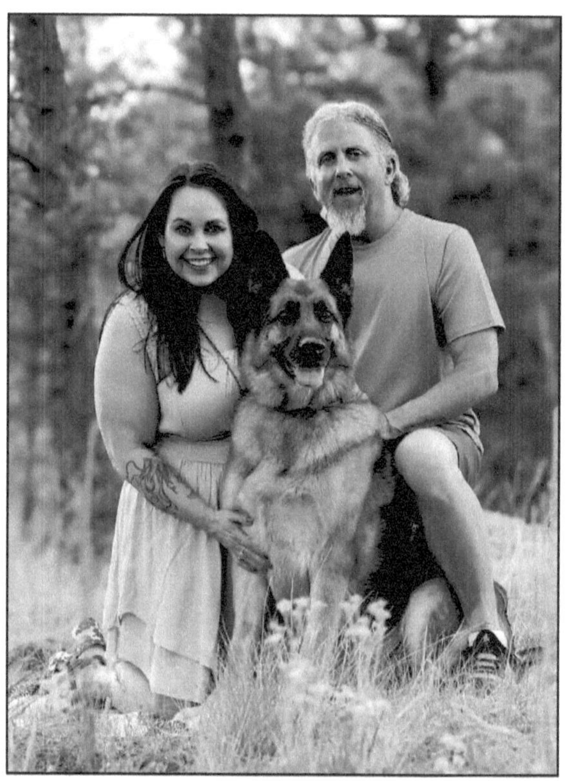

Here is a happy picture of Cosmo, smiling to encourage you
to care for your heart as you read this book!

THE TRUTH MIGHT BE HARD TO SWALLOW

Trafficking is real, and it is happening all around us every day. It's actually happening right here, in towns and cities all over the U.S. and across the globe. It's not a conspiracy theory or a Hollywood action flick. People are being trafficked in the communities we live in, at the places we work, at our kids' schools, and anywhere there is a way for enterprising traffickers to contact and communicate with vulnerable people.

You are reading this book because you want to know the *truth* about human trafficking. And I'm going to tell you nothing but the truth in the pages of this book. Because you're reading this book, you'll be able to identify the ways traffickers *target, groom, and exploit* their victims. As I share my real-life experiences, you'll learn how vulnerable people can be protected from these master manipulators. And if you read through till the end, you will discover tips and tools you need in order to become part of ending human trafficking.

My Mix of Motivating Factors

I'm Sandy Storm, and I was a human trafficking victim for twenty years, starting at just six years old. I experienced trafficking in many forms over those two decades, and I survived for a reason—to tell *you* the truth about human trafficking. Now, I am sharing my story—insider information—to help you protect the vulnerable people in your community. This story is raw and at times may be hard to read, but this story is real.

As a human trafficking survivor, I am an unfortunate expert on the ways traffickers think, act, and operate. As someone who was caught in cycles of victimization over and over again for two decades, I can help you understand the vulnerabilities traffickers seek to exploit for their own financial gain. And, as someone who has worked in the counter-trafficking arena since 2009, I can tell you what actions are most important and effective in ending human trafficking and what actions are a waste of resources, time, and energy.

Today, I am using my lived experience, specialized skillset, and unique expertise to dismantle the evil trafficking industry. As a certified coach, I have become a trusted advisor and trainer for professionals in many fields, including law enforcement, military intelligence, special operations, medical and mental health, education, social services, and faith-based organizations.

From my experience, whether serving a nonprofit or advising a government administration, I can confidently say no one organization or agency can singlehandedly provide a solution to end trafficking. My career began as a volunteer, and I have served in many capacities, including a four-year stint in an executive leadership position with a nonprofit, private intelligence agency. Within this organization, I daily worked shoulder-to-shoulder with former intelligence professionals from the NSA, CIA, FBI, and Navy SEALS. We brought the brightest minds together in a concerted effort to equip, train, and advise law enforcement around the world to identify, arrest, and prosecute traffickers. This was rewarding work, but there is still much more to be done; multitudes of professionals need to be trained on the truth about trafficking so we can bring an end to this global crime. That's why I am making this information available to you.

You might work in law enforcement, the military, or the medical field, or maybe you're a mental health professional or someone who works with at-risk populations within the education system or social services. Perhaps you're a parent, grandparent, foster care provider, or caregiver for vulnerable children. You may even work directly with trafficking survivors, or you could be a survivor yourself. Whatever your background, training, or experience, I want you to be encouraged knowing that we can work together to bring an end to the evil of trafficking that affects so many people.

Lightbulb Moments

In 2009, when I began volunteering with an anti-trafficking nonprofit, my passion for people was my inspiration. After learning about the ways trafficking was destroying lives, I felt responsible to offer my time, talent, and treasure to raise awareness and educate our community about this crime.

At first, I organized film screenings and presentations in coffee shops and partnered with local businesses and nonprofits to host events and gather resources. A few years later, after I had watched several documentaries, read many books about the issue, and heard dozens of stories from survivors, I had my own "lightbulb moment." Memories of desperate situations I had experienced flooded my mind, and I was able to connect the dots and see the patterns emerging. This is when I realized that I had been a victim of human trafficking.

Before that revelation, I would have referred to my experiences as molestation, rape, and domestic violence, but once I realized the common factor was another person profiting from my exploitation, I saw the indicators and was able to identify my experiences as trafficking. As you'll read when I share my story later in the book, I had stacks of medical records and piles of court documents that validated these experiences as trafficking. At first, I unpacked the memories as I confided in my husband, a counselor, and some close friends. I didn't share my story with the public for years.

Now, I'm building my kingdom on the skulls of my enemies.

Today, I'm using everything I learned in the training ground of my trauma to expose the evil I suffered and teach people who can do something about it how to go after the traffickers and set people free. Over the years, I have had the privilege of engaging directly with survivors, the honor of working with law enforcement on undercover investigations, and the blessing of sitting in courtrooms to see justice being served when traffickers were put behind bars, where they belonged.

The most rewarding part of my work has been watching thousands of people just like you have "lightbulb moments" as you become aware of the reality of trafficking and learn ways that you can play a part in solving this problem and bringing an end to slavery.

Human Trafficking, Defined

The crime of human trafficking is shaped around a business model that creates an illicit marketplace. Laws against slavery and human trafficking are on the books of nearly every nation on the planet; however, with estimates of nearly fifty million people[1] currently enslaved through labor trafficking, sexual slavery, debt bondage, or forced marriage, these laws are not being enforced to ensure justice prevails.

My definition of human trafficking is "the buying and selling of bodies and souls." Many people refer to this evil as "modern-day slavery." Other terms related to crimes of trafficking include the industry of commercial sexual exploitation, domestic servitude, child sexual abuse materials (previously referred to as child pornography), illegal organ trafficking, forced prostitution, nonconsensual image-based exploitation, child labor, and industrialized rape.

The U.S. Department of State has devoted resources to providing information to the public regarding the crime of human trafficking. Their definition states:

INTRODUCTION

"Trafficking in persons" and "human trafficking" are umbrella terms—often used interchangeably—to refer to a crime whereby traffickers exploit and profit at the expense of adults or children by compelling them to perform labor or engage in commercial sex. When a person younger than 18 is used to perform a commercial sex act, it is a crime regardless of whether there is any force, fraud, or coercion involved.[2]

According to the website of the U.S. Department of Justice:

> Human trafficking, also known as trafficking in persons, is a crime that involves compelling or coercing a person to provide labor or services, or to engage in commercial sex acts. The coercion can be subtle or overt, physical or psychological. Exploitation of a minor for commercial sex is human trafficking, regardless of whether any form of force, fraud, or coercion was used.[3]

The National Center for Missing and Exploited Children (NCMEC), which has been involved in the fight against child abuse and exploitation for many years, says:

> Child sex trafficking is a form of child abuse that occurs when a child under 18 is advertised, solicited or exploited through a commercial sex act. A commercial sex act is any sex act where something of value—such as money, food, drugs or a place to stay—is given to or received by any person for sexual activity.[4]

These definitions mean that for the crime of trafficking to be committed, a perpetrator influences or manipulates another person to exchange sexual contact or content for money or other resources. For example, suppose the traffickers are trapping their victims in a sweatshop. In that case, they might have presented a young man from another nation with what seemed like a legitimate job offer, including a work visa in the

U.S., but once he arrived, his new bosses withheld his documents, keeping him from seeking legal help. Imagine the difficulty of escaping this situation. Even if he's somehow able to break free and contact law enforcement, if the young man can't speak the language, he's unable to ask for help. And if his traffickers have possession of his immigration documents, the victim could fear the risk of imprisonment and deportation, especially if he's unaware of the T-Visa program.[5]

What these statements also denote is that, regarding situations involving sexual content or contact in any form, anyone under the age of eighteen engaged in commercial sex is classified by federal law as a victim of trafficking. One example of this would be an adult man pretending to be a 13-year-old kid in an online video game so he can communicate with a preteen girl, and then tricking her into producing and sending illegal images of herself in exchange for game credits. These criminals are especially deviant and often carry on conversations with many children at once to increase the probability of obtaining illicit images of minors.

In this nation, we see children as vulnerable people who need to be protected, and they are not able to give consent to a commercial transaction in exchange for access to their bodies, whether in person or through a video or image. In other words, there is no such thing as a child prostitute.

Reading definitions from governmental agencies can help define a crime in legal or technical terms, but for an everyday person to truly grasp the reality of a situation like human trafficking, it helps to hear true stories of real events. As a trafficking survivor, I believe God has given me this story, as well as the ability to tell it, for a reason—and He is not going to waste it. I survived the nightmare to share my story with you, so you can have a "lightbulb moment" of your own.

You might be asking, *How can an ordinary person make a difference in ending human trafficking? What can I do in my community to make sure it's a healthy, safe space for vulnerable people?* This book is packed with revelations on the TRUTH about trafficking and some practical actions you can take to safeguard the vulnerable and create protection from criminal traffickers. By the time you turn the last page, you'll be empowered to shine a light on this dark world of exploitation, and you'll be encouraged to share the hope of a life set free after you read my story of survival. *You* can be part of the solution to bringing an end to human trafficking.

Cut Through the Hype

There are stories in the news and online every day about traffickers and pedophiles, but the media seems to focus on sensationalism, division, and drama.

Wealthy, famous people were flying on a private jet to an exclusive island to be massaged by topless teen girls in the case involving Jeffrey Epstein, Ghislaine Maxwell, Prince Andrew, and countless popular celebrities. In another ring of deviance and depravity, witnesses told twisted tales of "freak-off" parties filled with abuse and exploitation in the federal courtroom regarding accused trafficker, music mogul Sean "Diddy" Combs, and his famous network. And in a scandal rocking the church community, Gateway megachurch founder and multi-millions-earning pastor Robert Morris, who has confessed to a "moral failure" he refers to as "inappropriate sexual behavior with a young lady," pled guilty to child sex crimes and was sentenced to serve six months of a suspended ten years in Oklahoma for lewd and indecent acts with a child beginning when she was only 12 years old.[6]

These stories involve celebrities and unimaginable wealth, but trafficking and exploitation also happen at all economic levels. What these flashy tales don't tell you is how this evil of trafficking is actually part of a business model. Whether they are doing their dealing in high-class resorts surrounded by high-end luxuries or at dirty dive motels on sketchy street corners, one thing is common with all traffickers—they are motivated by money. One trafficker may be blackmailing a well-known politician with photos of an encounter he had with a teen girl, while another trafficker is putting his victim out on "the track" to earn a $20 hit of dope. Sometimes there are many people involved with the cover-ups of the abuse and exploitation, incentivized into silence by all the money that's being made. At the end of the day, the traffickers will collect the profits, paid for by another person's exploitation.

When you understand how traffickers *target, groom, and exploit* their victims, you'll start seeing the signs in the city or town you live in, and you'll be better equipped to protect vulnerable people from becoming a part of this evil enterprise. You won't fall for the lies of Hollywood blockbusters or high-dollar PR agencies trying to spin the latest scandal to protect their celebrity clients. They can make it hard to see the red flags and subtle signs traffickers display, which is why I'm revealing their sneaky methods and sly tactics in the pages of this book.

In the first three chapters, you will be presented with the details of many specific strategies human traffickers use against their victims. I'll expose the dirty underbelly of the disturbing practice of human trafficking, and you will discover priceless frameworks that will help you to understand the ways traffickers are operating in your community.

Starting in chapter 4, I will unpack my story of survival, and we will go on a journey through two decades of abuse and exploitation. I will share true stories of many of the trafficking situations I experienced. This insider knowledge will be a crucial tool to help you learn the ways traffickers work. By knowing how my abusers trafficked me, you will see that victims oftentimes trust their traffickers because they are a parent, a perceived boyfriend, or someone else they mistakenly believe is trustworthy.

LIGHTBULB MOMENT

When you know the TRUTH about Human Trafficking, you'll see the tricks traffickers use to *target, groom, and exploit* people in an illicit marketplace.

INTRODUCTION

My story will help you understand how traffickers target victims who have a vulnerability that the trafficker exploits, like drug addiction, homelessness, or poverty. And, as in my situation, sometimes victims are coerced into selling sex once their resistance is broken down—whether because of deep wounds from childhood sexual abuse or perhaps after they start working in strip clubs or making pornography.

Despite the complex web of abuse and exploitation they have experienced, many trafficking victims are capable of breaking free to build a new life, so I always weave the truth about trafficking with threads of hope, even when sharing the darkest parts of my story. Not everyone makes it out of a trafficker's grip, but we have to hold onto hope that trafficking will end and the victims will all be able to heal. There are still so many trapped in cycles of exploitation, and without hope, they will never be free.

The sad truth is victims like me often fail to self-identify and therefore remain trapped, not because we were kidnapped and chained to a bed, but because we knew and trusted our traffickers or felt like it was our fault we were in the situation. Some victims may have been exploited by someone who should be fighting for them, like a cop, judge, pastor, or parent. And when we hear about trafficking in movies, on social media, or covered by the news, the stories are often unbelievable, involving celebrity scandals, kidnappings in parking lots, or romanticized tales of fantastic, faraway places. As you read my story, you'll understand how hard it can be to see the truth, even when you're living through the middle of it.

By understanding the **TRUTH** about trafficking, we will uncover the ways traffickers exploit vulnerabilities, discover how trafficking is happening in every community, discern the economic drivers of supply and demand at play, expose the tricks traffickers use to lure and manipulate their victims, and ultimately become better equipped to protect the vulnerable people in our communities.

Know the TRUTH:

Think about how traffickers *exploit* vulnerabilities for their own financial gain.

Realize that trafficking is happening *in your community.*

Understand the *supply & demand* driving the illicit trafficking market.

Track the tricks and traps traffickers use to *target, groom, and exploit* victims.

Help the vulnerable people in your community *stay safe!*

Knowing the **TRUTH** will set you free, so you can be a part of the solution. We can end human trafficking in our lifetime.

---

[1] Walk Free. "Global Slavery Index." https:// www.walkfree.org.
[2] U.S. Department of State. "Understanding Human Trafficking." January 20, 2025. https://www.state.gov/what-is-trafficking-in-persons/.
[3] U.S. Department of Justice. "What is Human Trafficking?" June 26, 2023. https://www.state.gov/what-is-trafficking-in-persons/.
[4] National Center for Missing and Exploited Children. "Child Sex Trafficking." https://www.missingkids.org/theissues/trafficking.
[5] U. S. Citizenship and Immigration Services. "Victims of Human Trafficking: T Nonimmigrant Status." https://www.uscis.gov/humanitarian/victims-of-human-trafficking-t-nonimmigrant-status
[6] https://www.usatoday.com/story/news/2025/10/02/robert-morris-gateway-church-founder-child-sex-crimes-plea-oklahoma/86463485007/

PART ONE

Exposing the Disturbing Practice of Trafficking

Chapter 1

TARGETED
Finding the Perfect Victim

A young mom pushes her shopping cart through a suburban SuperTarget store. She is in "the zone," finding bargains, sniffing new candle scents, and helping her almost-two-year-old swipe through YouTube videos of silly songs and bright cartoons on an iPad. The blonde-haired, blue-eyed little boy is strapped into the front of the buggy seat, cheerily staring at the screen as mommy shops to her heart's content.

As they turn a corner, the mom sees two men, possibly of Middle Eastern or maybe South American descent, talking to each other in a foreign language. These men are dressed in black, and they seem to be looking at her and her child, giving her an eerie feeling. She turns the corner and heads up a different aisle, and again, the two men are chattering and seem to conveniently be in the same place she is, no matter which way she turns.

This mom is scared and feels like she and her son are being targeted. She heads to the front of the store and pulls her child from the cart, leaving behind the items she intended to purchase. Rushing to her SUV, conveniently parked in a space near the front of the store, Mom straps her toddler into the car seat and jumps in the driver's seat. She backs up and pulls away from the store as the mysterious men emerge and defeatedly throw their hands in the air. This suburbanite has foiled their nefarious plan.

Once her baby in the backseat is asleep and she can regain her composure, the mom pulls over at a park where she positions her vehicle in front of the playground. She lowers her visor and opens the vanity mirror, illuminating tiny LED lights to cast a flattering glow on her face as she digs her lipstick and mascara out of her purse. After touching up her makeup and running a brush through her glossy hair, she adjusts the neckline of her blouse and straightens the diamond-encrusted cross pendant hanging from a gold chain around her neck.

Once she feels confident and "camera-ready," she pulls out her smartphone. After typing a short, attention-grabbing caption into her favorite social media channel, she flips the switch to go live, streaming a video available to be viewed by her thousands of followers at once. The mom tells of the events of her harrowing afternoon as her child sleeps in the car seat behind her and other moms push their kids on the swings that can be seen through the rear window of her vehicle.

"These men were sex traffickers, and if I hadn't been paying attention, they would have kidnapped my baby to sell on the dark web!" she cries into her phone's camera, her eyes welling with tears.

With the rapt followers and fans hanging on her every word, she sees messages of support, shock, and sympathy from her connections as they post hearts and other emojis on the live feed. As the mom tells the tale of being stalked and hunted by these dangerous foreigners, she warns the crowd to stay alert and aware. Her message is clear to those listening—sex trafficking can happen to anyone, anywhere. Even at Target! Even on an otherwise ordinary afternoon. Even to a suburban-social-media-influencer-mom like her.

The likes, loves, comments, and public show of support explode on her post. Comments start blowing up from her frightened audience members wanting to know which Target she was shopping at so they could avoid that store and the entire neighborhood. People desperate for more details frantically type in their questions: What did the men say to her? What were they wearing? Did she see the car they got into? Did she get a license plate number?

The excitement and commotion cause her child to wake from his blissful nap, and the mom starts wrapping up her live feed to tend to her little one. She reminds everyone to stay safe, thanks them for their support in this tragic situation, and casually mentions that if they want to continue supporting her channel and her choice to be a stay-at-home momma and #girlboss, they can sign up to get the product she markets through a popular direct sales company. She tells them that this will help her be their eyes and ears on the street while they work their nine-to-five jobs, but if they ever want to take the leap and start their own home-based business, she can help them get started right away.

Finally, she reminds the viewers that there is no safe place for their children and encourages them to take control of their lives. Her advice is that they find ways to spend more time with their kids to keep them safe from evil traffickers lurking in grocery aisles and parking lots. And the company she represents could be the solution they need to make that dream of working from home a reality.

Once she turns off the camera, the post keeps going. The momentum builds quickly, and while dozens watch the live feed, hundreds quickly view and share the video, and within the hour, it has thousands of views, reactions, and shares. This is her viral moment, and the publicity leads to her network exploding as she adds some new customers and even more people showing interest in her business opportunity.

Is this mom a hero, or is she part of the problem?

The Cold, Hard Truth

From my extensive research and years of collaboration with law enforcement across the country and in other parts of the world, there have been no confirmed cases of sex trafficking from women with small children being followed through a grocery store and snatched from a parking lot.

Traffickers likely would not stalk a confident woman and try to kidnap her or her children because it is too risky. A screaming mother would put up a fight and cause a scene if her kid was snatched, so a trafficker would rather find an "easy" target like a teen runaway or a single mom who is desperate and vulnerable. Traffickers want to put forth as little effort as possible and make it seem like their victims chose that life; that is how they control them.

A big misconception is that a predator targeting kids is a creepy stranger who is driving around in a big white van, handing out free candy to trick a child into getting into the vehicle, then locking the doors and speeding off down the road. A modern, more realistic scenario usually involves a trusted person who already has access to the child, like a family member, teacher, coach, church leader, or another adult in a position of authority in the child's life.

For example, fatherless families are filled with vulnerabilities. Daughters growing up without the love and defense of a daddy, sons being raised without a strong example of a provider, and single moms struggling to make ends meet—these difficult realities create an opportunity for a trafficker to infiltrate the home and provide false hope, drawing the unprotected into a web of deceit and exploitation.

This is one of many reasons why single moms are targets for traffickers. Traffickers know they can leverage their distress, play on their desperation to gain trust, and convince them to do things these moms would have never done without their influence and manipulation. For instance, when a mother is desperate to put food on the table or get the necessary cash to pay rent or utility bills, she is vulnerable to a trafficker swooping in to save the day. After my father died, my mother was targeted by a trafficker who promised to provide and care for her and her children, but instead, he exploited me.

LIGHTBULB MOMENT

 **Trafficking victims aren't usually snatched off the street by strangers; they often know and trust their traffickers.**

The situation described at the beginning of this chapter is fictional, but it is based on real posts by influencers and other social groups. Videos like these are offensive to anyone who has ever been trafficked. It is derisive and insulting that she would sensationalize her story to get likes and shares when there are victims suffering torture, rape, abuse, and other horrific circumstances while they are being trafficked. But the mom in this story has a real reason to post a sensational video. She wants to go viral—she wants to sell, sell, sell her product, so she is jumping on the latest trend to push her video onto everyone's feed. Please don't help people like this push their agendas; they truly are part of the problem.

Innocent kids deserve to be safe and protected from criminal traffickers, and it starts by knowing the risk factors traffickers target. We need not worry about every scary white van in the grocery store parking lot. (However, sometimes those vans might indeed belong to bad people, so it's still a good practice to stay aware of our surroundings.)

Traffickers usually spend time and money building a relationship of trust with their potential victims. This means the lines are blurred whether the victim perceives family ties, a romantic bond, or a business partnership. The traffickers often target their victims using a systematic approach, and when you have your eyes open to see how it really happens, social media myths like the Target story won't distract you from the truth.

Do you know what child trafficking looks like in your community?
The traffickers know.
The buyers know.
And the victims know.

But somehow, it happens right on the other side of the curtain of our polite society.

Traffickers have an advantage today because they don't have to sneak through locked doors to snatch sleeping victims from their beds. For the first time in history, due to advances in technology, a conniving criminal anywhere in the world has the opportunity to contact and connect directly with a young, vulnerable, potential victim at any time—day or night—by using social media, chat applications, and video game consoles.

These traffickers can now *target, groom, and exploit* their victims without ever even meeting them in person. And the victims might be carrying a communication device with them at all times, causing them to feel trapped in the exploitative cycle with no hope of breaking free. Plus, the gadgets we use to communicate have a way of creating an illusion of deep, personal connection; these predators know that kids are often alone in their bedrooms playing video games or holding their phones in their hands, intensely focused on the devices in front of them.

Imagine if these conversations happen after lights out, when a kid is supposed to be asleep and tech devices are supposed to be stored away. That creates an additional obstacle that can prevent the victim from reaching out to a parent or trusted adult for help, not wanting to get in trouble for breaking the rules.

Before the digital age, parents and caregivers would tell their kids about "stranger danger." Years ago, teenage children could be left home alone and told not to open the door if anyone knocked or not to answer the phone if it rang. Today, the only thing keeping a predator from targeting a young person is a "digital door" that offers virtually no protection. With that door essentially wide open, the traffickers can leverage technology to reach out to many targets at once, increasing their odds of finding new victims to scale their operations.

This opportunity for traffickers to secretly target children has given them the advantage, and they have very little risk involved. It's important to equip young people with information and tools to help lower the odds that they will become victims, but it's equally important to know how the criminals are masterminding the building of their illicit businesses.

Drawing the Target

Traffickers will spend a lot of time, money, and resources to **FIND** a vulnerable target they can groom and exploit. Here's how it often plays out:

Targeting

How Traffickers FIND the Perfect Victim

Focus—The trafficker zeroes in on the potential target.

Investigate—The trafficker begins to gather information and intelligence about the potential victim.

Notice—The trafficker analyzes the opportunity, looking for any cracks to get through.

Develop or Detour—If favorable, the trafficker takes things to the next level. If the victim is not found to be an optimal target, the trafficker will abandon the pursuit to find a "better" option for a potential victim.

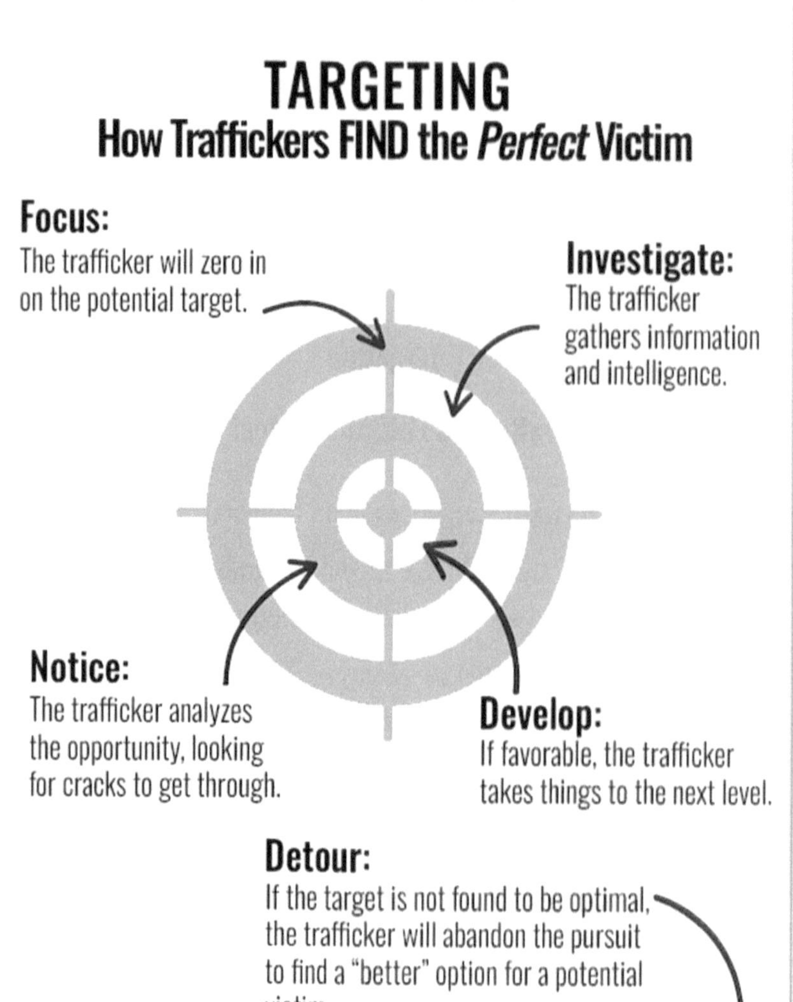

Focus

Whether traffickers are hunting for potential victims online, in their local church, or through the personal connections and relationships they have with parents or guardians of young children, they usually have a specific victim profile in mind. Some traffickers look for young, prepubescent children, while others seek teenagers. Some traffickers specifically target people with active drug addictions, those facing financial instability, or desperate people in desperate situations, like being homeless or having a developmental disability. Some traffickers intentionally avoid targeting anyone underage because they know the punishment will be more severe if they are prosecuted.

The work a trafficker puts into finding a target might look like scrolling on social media or swiping through a dating app, or it could mean showing up to junior high baseball games or high school soccer practices to survey the scene. These crafty criminals usually don't look like bad guys or dangerous girls, but instead, they often hold positions of trust and authority in the community. They might have access to at-risk people because they volunteer at a school or church, or they might have jobs working with vulnerable persons seeking support services.

When finding new victims, traffickers frequently target victims of childhood abuse and neglect. They might seek people who have low self-esteem because such people are often easier to manipulate and groom. Abuse victims may see themselves as damaged goods, and they often have weak boundaries, making them prime targets for traffickers. If a trafficker can weaponize the abuse and use it as a tool to motivate his victim, he can program his victim to remain in that dysfunctional cycle to the benefit of the trafficker, who will collect all the profits.

When I was a vulnerable young adult, traffickers saw my trauma as an opportunity and focused on me as a target. They saw me as someone who had already been trained to accept abuse, to accept whatever was done to my body because that's what I thought I deserved.

It is not hard for traffickers to find a victim, especially when a common theme in trafficking cases is that the victim trusts the trafficker. This is usually because the trafficker seems like someone who *should* be trustworthy, like a close relative, family friend, or a romantic interest. The trafficker might be someone the victim sees as a provider of support and protection, like a teacher, pastor, coach, politician, or local business leader.

These traffickers have an advantage of being trusted not only by the victim but often by the community as well.

Investigate

Traffickers not only gather as much information as they can on a potential victim, but they often research anyone and everyone in that victim's life. They attempt to build a knowledge base that they will later exploit.

This fact-finding can happen in a matter of minutes by searching the online footprint of a potential target through social media content, photos, friends and family connections, and other interests. What traffickers know—but many people don't realize—is that when adults make posts on social media with pictures of their family, an abundance of information is made available to a discerning investigator with a critical eye. In a similar way to how a police detective will assemble a case by analyzing a criminal's "digital fingerprints," a trafficker who knows how to decipher subtle clues can uncover detailed information, including home addresses, the names of a child's school and sports teams, and the routines the child might be involved in, like music lessons at the mall on Tuesday afternoons.

It is too easy for a trafficker to squeeze details from a vulnerable person he is targeting. These criminals hunt for broken people to leverage the instability and insecurities these individuals are facing, ultimately manipulating their victims into sharing crucial information that could put them in danger. It's not difficult for a sly trafficker to trick his potential victim into disclosing details that will help him figure out whether or not the victim has a strong supporter who might try to step in to offer protection.

Another tactic traffickers might engage in is asking a lot of personal questions, putting up a façade to appear interested in the hopes and desires of their target. This not only quickly builds the perceived relationship deeper, but it also gives the trafficker information that will be used against the target in the future. While they are digging for this intimate knowledge, the traffickers might disguise themselves as a caring friend or a lonely misfit to play on their potential victim's sympathies and continue to build trust in the relationship, thus beginning the grooming process.

Notice

If there are cracks to get through, traffickers take notice and make strategic and calculated plans to break through barriers to build a deeper connection of trust with the target they have in their crosshairs. Some of the openings they might look for include:

- a history of abuse,
- a lack of strong, healthy relationships with parents or authority figures,
- experience with sexual situations,
- exposure to pornography,
- drug and alcohol abuse or dependence, and
- a lack of a support system, reliable housing, or financial stability.

Traffickers' targets are often people who are young and naive about how the world works. Armed with this knowledge, these criminals will seek out any indicators they can find that reveal a vulnerability they might be able to exploit.

Simply put, traffickers exploit vulnerabilities. I can say from first-hand experience that traffickers exploit people who have been victims of abuse by honing in on their need for provision, guidance, and love. They often seek fatherless children from broken families and use their desire for protection and guidance as a way to groom them into trusting that the trafficker cares for them or will be a father figure to them. I was a victim of abuse, and the traffickers saw the indications, then exploited me for their own financial gain.

It's like we have signs on our foreheads saying, "I'm vulnerable." Predators see that sign and cycle in and out of our broken lives, taking advantage of us every chance they get.

Develop or *Detour*

Traffickers will assess the situation after gathering information and looking for cracks in a target's life. If the situation appears favorable, the trafficker will take things to the next level by engaging in more significant relationship-building. If they determine they have not found an optimal target, they will abandon the pursuit to find a "better" option for a potential victim. It is not uncommon for traffickers to have multiple targets they are assessing at any given time, and they can easily switch their attention and focus toward someone who presents a more lucrative money-making opportunity.

LIGHTBULB MOMENT

 **Safe, healthy homes for kids to grow up in can be a defense against trafficking.**

Traffickers try to isolate victims so they feel like they can't talk to anyone about what's going on behind the scenes. This is why it is so important to prepare children to be protected and shielded from predators, and it is equally important to educate the young people in our lives about the reality of the evil that exists in our world. Predators are counting on their targets to be naive and trusting, so we must equip kids with the tools and knowledge they need to keep them aware of the dangers they could be facing.

Vulnerable people need to have safe, healthy relationships with people they can count on. They need to know someone cares for them and that they have someone trustworthy to talk to about anything. That's how safety nets are built to protect vulnerable people.

When kids have a trusted adult—someone they can always come to for help in navigating difficult situations and uncomfortable conversations—they can be confident that the safe person they confide in will protect and guide them. Even if they have broken a rule or been disobedient by talking on instant messenger with strangers or playing a video game after they were supposed to have lights off and technology put away, they will have someone to open up to and come clean to. That way, if the young person ends up in a situation where someone is pressuring them to send inappropriate images or to meet up in real life, she will have someone to help her handle that difficult circumstance and protect her from getting drawn further away from safety and stability.

When we teach kids how to have safe relationships and caution them on the dangers of online predators, we are making them bad targets for traffickers. This protects them from traffickers developing relationships with them and luring them into the next phase of the illicit operation, grooming, which we will discuss in greater detail in the next chapter.

A Word About Prevention

I have a controversial view of prevention when it comes to the anti-trafficking work that many organizations claim to engage in. While it is an important undertaking to teach young, vulnerable people about the dangers that exist in our world in hopes of preventing them from becoming targets of predators, the emphasis in many "prevention" programs is misguided.

Imagine there being a growing issue in the city where you live involving pedestrians being struck by cars. What a disaster it would be if the campaign around awareness and preventing pedestrians from being injured focused only on teaching innocent walkers to watch out for cars driving on the sidewalks or simply telling pedestrians to stay out of traffic. That might cut down on some injuries, but a better focus would be on educating reckless drivers on how destructive their choices can be. Leveraging large fines for driving on walkways and punishing drivers who don't obey traffic laws would be a more effective prevention method in this example.

In the anti-trafficking space, frequent offerings geared toward prevention include self-defense classes and awareness training for at-risk populations. Those presentations might be helpful to increase confidence or bolster self-esteem, but they are doing little to prevent trafficking. When the focus shifts from potential vulnerable victims to the traffickers and buyers, we will begin making headway. Vulnerable people will always exist—another kid turns thirteen every day. The difference is made when we prevent someone from ever going down the criminal road of buying or selling another human being.

Unfortunately, there is an undercurrent in our modern age that minimizes the crime of purchasing people, and it makes it into a crude cultural joke. Pimps (traffickers) are portrayed as flashy and flamboyant figures in movies and music videos. Bachelor parties where women are rented (to be abused) are kept as secrets between frat brothers holding to the creed: "What happens in Vegas stays in Vegas." Dads celebrate their sons' eighteenth birthdays with lap dances or trips to brothels. And the common consumption of violent, degrading, on-demand, internet-streamed pornography is rising to become a public health crisis.[1]

Educating the buyers driving the demand about the harmful results of their choices is a more effective way of preventing trafficking than teaching people how not to get pimped out. Enforcing harsh penalties for anyone involved in the selling of a vulnerable person will prevent criminals from choosing this path in favor of a crime involving a less severe punishment.

If we want to stop trafficking, we collectively need to work to establish a society where putting a price tag on a person is viewed as the perverted practice it is.

A Glimpse into the Grooming Process

In the next chapter, we are going to unpack the methods traffickers use to groom their victims into submission. You will discover the ways these master manipulators with money motivations quickly gain trust, whether by becoming the Romeo or role-playing as a father figure. We will examine how traffickers can seem obsessed or overly involved with their victims, when behind the scenes, they are making calculated moves to exceed and remove boundaries. Often, victims will be unaware of the red flags that are waving because of the intoxicating methods traffickers use to indoctrinate them and make them compliant.

---

[1] Perdue, Mitzi, "Pornography: The Public Health Crisis of the Digital Age," Psychology Today, April 15, 2021, https://www.psychologytoday.com/us/blog/end-human-trafficking/202104/pornography-the-public-health-crisis-the-digital-age.

Chapter 2

GROOMING—BREAKING DOWN BOUNDARIES
How Traffickers Build Trust

In the summer of 2022, Ghislaine Maxwell was found guilty of federal charges of child sex trafficking involving recruiting, grooming, and abusing teen victims with her perverted partner, Jeffrey Epstein. She was sentenced to twenty years in a federal prison for her crimes of conspiring to abuse children.[1]

Exactly how did she get so many young girls to be part of this twisted, exploitative situation?

According to the United States attorney who prosecuted the case, Maxwell intentionally targeted particularly vulnerable, fatherless children and used manipulative tactics to persuade the girls to trust her. This glamorous socialite was charming and rich, and she promised these little 14-year-olds that they could have a lavish life of comfort, excess, and travel like she was living. The catch was that they would have to do something in exchange for the designer clothes, luxury items, or expensive educations that she dangled in front of them.

That "something" usually involved the child being alone in a room with a naked man who would tell them what they had to do. It might have been giving Jeffrey or one of his friends a massage, and it might have been doing more than just giving someone a rub-down. When there was more demanded of the victim than a simple massage, Ghislaine would assist in the abuse, normalizing the sexualization and creating the illusion that these interactions were a standard part of the therapeutic massage procedure.

Maxwell knew she increased her chances of finding victims by targeting girls from low-income, single-mother homes; these girls would likely be impressed by the allure of Epstein's opulent mansions, where they would come for the illicit encounters. After abusing the teens, the pair of predators would provide their naive victims with hundreds of dollars in cash, promising even more money if they recruited additional victims for the sordid ring of sexual perversion.

Epstein and Maxwell used these little girls to fulfill their sick fantasies and turned them into magnets to attract other teens from broken homes or with low self-esteem, allowing the duo to expand the scope of their crimes with victims spread across the nation and into other parts of the world. They had a deep pool of conditioned, trained, obedient schoolgirls who would act on command in exchange for a small token or meager financial reward.

In this sick, twisted case of wickedness, the grooming and the abuse were one and the same. Every time the couple or their associates assaulted a child, it further indoctrinated the victim into accepting the behavior as a normal procedure or something that should be expected during the encounter. And as the list of abuse victims grew, the money that flowed through the criminals' hands reached astronomical amounts, causing ripple effects that became a question of fiduciary responsibility for one of the world's oldest financial institutions.

The year after Maxwell was sent to prison, JP Morgan—at the time the largest bank in the U.S.—settled a lawsuit for $290 million to be paid to Epstein's victims.[2] The bank then settled another suit later that year, paying the Virgin Islands $75 million.[3] While under oath, JP Morgan's CEO, Jamie Dimon, issued what might be interpreted as an apology to the victims, saying, "And I wouldn't mind personally apologizing to them, not because we committed the crime, we did not, and not because we believe we're responsible."[4] Epstein had hundreds of millions spread in more than fifty accounts at JP Morgan, and the bank profited handsomely from the years of business they did with the criminal. In the next chapter, we will dive deeper into how the business of trafficking is hidden in plain sight, becoming intertwined with legal operations like the financial industry. But first, it's important that we understand fully the tactics these predators employ to break, condition, and groom their potential victims, so let's dive deeper into this topic.

Masters of Manipulation, Motivated by Money

Traffickers coerce and manipulate victims—without regard for human life—in the pursuit of making money by any means.

Not all traffickers are multimillionaires, and the grooming techniques traffickers use are as varied as the predators' profiles. Traffickers vary from moms who sell sexual contact with their children in exchange for drugs, to low-level thugs who act as pimps forcing vulnerable people into prostitution, to global networks of slave traders who transport their victims around the world. These criminals create an illicit marketplace network where a demand for trafficked individuals puts people at risk. To see behind the curtain of this shameless practice, we can look at the ways victims are brought from the targeting phase into a period of grooming, when they will be broken down.

The manipulation and mental programming can be as simple as expressing praise and giving compliments, or it may look like the trafficker rewarding compliance with small tokens, a drug supply, or cash. This is similar to the way you might train a dog—by giving treats, praise, and showing your approval for obedience. Once a victim has been conditioned to perform for the approval of his controller or unlock the reward that's being dangled in front of her, the trafficker knows there is no turning back. They've created a moneymaker, and the possibilities for profits are endless.

As traffickers build their corrupt business models, they are often simultaneously building bonds with their victims to establish trust and produce compliant, obedient slaves who will do as instructed without resistance, perform on command, and hand over all the money with no opposition. This is done through the grooming process.

LIGHTBULB MOMENT

Traffickers use the grooming process to destroy their victims' boundaries and build a bond that will be hard to break.

These enterprising criminals don't stop at merely grooming their victims, but they often groom the members of the support system who surround the targeted individual. If they can convince the community to believe that they are a trustworthy person, the victim will be less inclined to disclose details of the twisted exploitation happening behind closed doors. This is a type of institutional grooming that results from the misguided trust placed in someone merely because they hold a position of influence or authority over children or other vulnerable people. Remember, sometimes predators seek opportunities to volunteer with children or be in leadership positions over a vulnerable segment of the community, where they intend to abuse those in their care.

Traffickers manipulate their victims into situations that feel like choices, but the scales are always tipped in favor of the ones collecting all the money; they never benefit the person being sold. The mind games traffickers use to groom their targets can leave their victims with a distorted reality, blurry memories, and crumbling boundaries.

Broken Boundaries Build Business

Traffickers will often invest time, money, and energy to groom their victims into submission before they exploit them. Using flattery and showering their victims with gifts help the traffickers gain their victims' trust while they work to capitalize on their vulnerabilities.

When a trafficker spends money to groom the person she wants to exploit, the return on her investment is two-fold, starting with the compliance of her victim. The expenditure is a two-sided coin that benefits the trafficker twice: first, by placing a sense of obligation on the victim to repay the perceived kindness, and second, by providing the target with clothes, jewelry, or makeup that will later be used to advertise her to be sold on the market.

During the grooming process, a trafficker will typically attempt to lower the victim's inhibitions by gradually introducing sex into conversations or exposing her to pornography. Traffickers often desensitize potential victims to the taboos in the world of commercial sex through internet porn, stripping, or sex for sale through online outlets. When these acts are normalized, it becomes increasingly more difficult for the victim to enforce boundaries.

For example, traffickers love sites like PornHub and OnlyFans. These websites desensitize the victim to look at sex as a commodified activity. It trains the victim to receive money in exchange for the sex act, and all the trafficker has to do is convince the victim that he's a better manager of that money than the victim. As you'll read when I share the ways I was trained to perform on command, my traffickers used print and video-recorded pornographic media, specifically showing me X-rated images or movies, to desensitize me and train me to do what they wanted.

Enterprising traffickers use the lurid sex industry as a lure by showing their potential victims all the money available. The illusion of mountains of cash becomes a trap; the victim gets stuck in a downward spiral while the trafficker counts all the profits. The conditioning process normalizes the perverted acts and creates a snare, making it difficult for the victim to go back to an ordinary life after being exposed to the deviant world of sex for sale.

LIGHTBULB MOMENT

 **The industry of commercial sexual exploitation creates a slippery slope for vulnerable young women—It's easy to enter but can seem impossible to break free from the dehumanizing cycles of transactional sex.**

The truth is that the commercial sex industry feeds on the most vulnerable among us to survive. It steals from the poor to enrich the lives of abusive pimps. Traffickers target survivors of abuse and add to their trauma. Like me, most sex trafficking victims have a history of childhood sexual abuse. Traffickers use these and other vulnerabilities to groom their victims, keeping them from leaving or seeking help, thus continuing the corrupt and destructive cycle.

Many victims don't leave because they don't even realize they are being trafficked. Because the grooming methods can alter their perception of reality, trafficking victims rarely self-identify. The mental manipulation tactics traffickers use can confuse victims and cause them to believe the twisted situation they find themselves in is a result of their own choices. People who don't realize they are being manipulated can become partners in their abuse. This keeps the victim caught in the deceitful web and keeps the traffickers piling up the profits.

Violence and Threats as Tools of Control

Traffickers often control every aspect of their victims' lives, and free will is usually the first thing a trafficker strips away during the grooming process. When the trafficker is in a position of power and the victim is no longer in control, manipulation can easily lead to exploitation. Since a trafficker wants submissive victims who will perform on command and hand over all the money made, he first has to break his target down. This is how he exercises control and keeps his victims held by invisible chains.

Whether at the hands of a trafficker or a purchaser, victims of human trafficking often suffer abuse, assault, and exploitation in horrific ways. This causes a cycle of guilt and shame that keeps the victim bound to "the only one who understands" the many difficult things they have experienced together.

The domino effect of past abuse, neglect, and childhood trauma is compounded when traffickers torture, rape, beat, or starve their victims. These criminals may groom or force their victims to commit crimes, use drugs, or have abortions. Because traffickers often target those who have developed unhealthy reliance on substances or become addicted to alcohol or drugs as a way to cope with the nightmares they lived through as children, these circumstances may lead to the victims ending up with criminal records, further complicating any plans they may have to escape the situation the trafficker has them trapped in.

Remember: trafficking victims are often controlled and held captive not by chains or ropes tying them to a bed but by threats or violent acts committed against them or their loved ones. Victims often feel trapped in the situation because of their fear of being harmed or killed. Many traffickers use firearms and other weapons to threaten violence, then leverage fear to gain more control over the victims, and a vicious cycle ensues. According to the Bureau of Justice Statistics in an analysis of the nearly 3,000 human trafficking incidents reported by U.S. law enforcement in 2022:

> An estimated 12% of sex trafficking incidents and 14% of labor trafficking incidents involved a firearm. Personal weapons (including hands, fists, feet, arms, and teeth) were used in 59%

of sex trafficking incidents and 68% of labor trafficking incidents, more than any other weapon type.[5]

I have firsthand experience with the devastating effects of violence at the hands of these conniving criminals. My traffickers forced me to have an abortion when I was twelve years old, and later I had my head busted open by a pimp and my teeth kicked out by a man who enslaved me. These violent events were a seemingly normal part of my dysfunctional life, and because I had been meticulously groomed, I couldn't decipher the dangerous circumstances of the brutal situations I found myself in. I didn't have a network of a trusted support system, and the trauma became a regular way of life for me.

The Trap of Trauma

Trauma is a tricky thing. It both creates vulnerabilities and is a result of the exploitation of vulnerabilities.

Imagine you don't have the money to pay your rent, feed your children, or buy the medicine your family needs.

Now, imagine being in that desperate situation and someone tells you they can help you solve all your problems, but you'll have to experience the unthinkable trauma of repeated sexual assaults and endure the shame and stigma associated with those traumas.

If you had to choose between these two horrible situations, how would you decide what to do?

Trauma makes it hard to make healthy decisions. Exploitation often leads to desperation, and traffickers know that a desperate person could be willing to do anything just to survive. When a vulnerable young woman is exploited by a trafficker and groomed to sell herself, new layers of trauma become interwoven with the trauma that made her vulnerable in the first place.

This puts the exploiter—the trafficker—in a position of power and continues the unhealthy cycle until the victim is essentially trapped in the life, looking to the trafficker as her only source of provision and stability.

When everyone in your life is abusing you, it's hard to believe that anyone out there is on your side. This is a huge obstacle for victims to overcome and is one that often prevents them from seeking safety. If we can shift the collective mindset that creates stigma around this issue, we will make a safe space for victims to break free from the cycles of grooming and come out of hiding to seek healing and restoration.

Learning to be free is not an easy task for a trafficking victim. The invisible strings that tie a desperate person to an enterprising trafficker could be a sense of financial security, the need for acceptance and "family," or even the belief that it would be impossible to live a life any different from the familiar cycles of exploitation and victimization.

Nothing stings more than seeing the people who should be trying to save you add to your suffering. This can be a powerful tool in the hands of a manipulative trafficker. For example, an experience involving a police officer who victimizes a person in his lowest and most desperate place can cause a mental barrier to form so that the victim will not trust police, even if he encounters agents or officers who are attempting to help him escape the dangerous traps of his traffickers. He may voluntarily choose to remain in the control of his trafficker because of his overwhelming fear of police.

Love-Bombs and Trauma Bonds

Sometimes, the hardest chains to break are psychological ones. Human trafficking victims are often violated by people they know and should be able to count on and trust. As we have discussed, traffickers groom their victims, keeping them virtually enslaved with the invisible chains of threats, violence, fear, addiction, verbal abuse, emotional blackmail, physical isolation, mind control, and manipulation. But one of the most powerful tools traffickers have at their disposal is the rollercoaster of love.

Have you ever been so in love that you felt like you had butterflies in your belly, and all you could think of all day and night was your love interest? There is science behind those feelings of infatuation. Falling in love causes a release of a powerful "love hormone" called oxytocin, and engaging in sexual activity increases the flow of this bonding biochemical through the bloodstream.

Even the illusion of love can evoke intoxicating emotions, and traffickers act as master manipulators who use their victims' hormonal responses to create powerful instinctive reactions, gaining control over the minds of their targets. Traffickers might shower a teen girl by "love bombing" her with affection to release the feel-good hormones, then quickly switch to anger and abuse to cause her fight-or-flight response system to activate. When the victim is suddenly seized by fear, her body will dump adrenaline and cortisol into the already flooded nervous system. This causes a cascading effect of a chemical cocktail to rage through her body. These cycles of peaks and valleys can seem like an intoxicating drug to her, and it can become addictive to experience the intense highs and lows.[6]

LIGHTBULB MOMENT

Traffickers sometimes groom their victims by showering them with love then suddenly becoming violent, setting off a cascading chemical reaction that releases an intoxicating cocktail of hormones, which creates a powerful trauma bond.

Trauma bonds are often formed around severely distressing situations, and the manipulation and mind control tactics traffickers use continuously chip away at the autonomy of their victims. Traffickers know that the more these hormones are manipulated and falsely coaxed into release, the less they are available for natural distribution. That means the victim will eventually start to crave the emotions of fear and terror produced by the trafficker's outbursts of anger. In the same manner, the victim will crave the serotonin and epinephrine released when the trafficker speaks kindly or lovingly. This kind of physical reliance forms a powerful connection between the victim and trafficker.

This is an emotional attachment that results from a repeated cycle of abuse followed immediately by a positive reinforcement. The manipulation of a victim's trauma response and the release of endorphins create hormonal triggers, resulting in a programmed physiological and psychological response to the recurring, cyclical abusive patterns.

This powerful effect can make it impossible to differentiate abuse from love and often causes victims to become party to their own exploitation. I know all too well that the bonds that keep victims tied to their traffickers typically are not tangible but are constructed within the mind of the victim through the trafficker's manipulation and abuse.

Traffickers often work to keep their victims isolated from their friends, family, and society as a whole, so finding help is especially difficult in these cases. Destroying the relationships with anyone who might help them break free is a strategy predators use to strengthen the bond they are building with their victims. You'll see in my story—isolation is a part of the grooming process.

False Father Figures

Traffickers are only as powerful as the lies they convince their victims to believe. By using deception and manipulation, they persuade the victim to stay trapped in destructive situations. These traffickers might present themselves as safety nets, managers, or sugar daddies who care about their girls, depending on what they say during the recruiting and grooming process. As the traffickers initiate the illicit encounters, their victims are broken down and become accustomed to the patterns of abuse and exploitation, eventually accepting their fate as they stop resisting or putting up a fight. In this way, the trafficking acts as a continuation of the grooming process.

Men seeking access to young children they can traffic and abuse might seek out single mothers of young children. They know that without a dad to protect and provide for the kids, the grooming process can be condensed, allowing them to quickly get down to business. Sometimes the trafficker will present himself as a romantic interest for the mother, all the while cunningly grooming the children to later be exploited. Or he might serve as a youth pastor or as a mentor to at-risk youth through a volunteer service, acting as a concerned father-figure, only to gain the trust of both child and mother so he can eventually have his way and abuse the trusting teen.

Strip clubs are infamous for making money off of girls with "daddy issues." These predatory businesses present vulnerable, "barely legal" young women with a structured environment where they are put on display to be praised and rewarded for their performance by older men who flaunt their wealth and flash their cash. The club managers will actively hunt for girls who lack the guidance and approval of a trusted male guardian. This means there is a lower likelihood of someone talking her out of working at the strip club. Plus, the club will make money from the steady stream of men looking to buy access to a vulnerable girl who lacks the guidance and direction of a concerned dad.

Playing the Part of the Romantic Romeo

Traffickers want "willing victims" who will turn in all the money they make without putting up resistance. They usually aren't inclined to take a big risk; they are looking for easy money.

One of the most common tactics traffickers use to trick their victims into compliance is the "Romeo Pimp" model—they shower a young person with gifts, attention, and affection, making them believe they're in love. And once they have their victim under that intoxicating spell, they manipulate the victim into doing things she otherwise would not have done.

Traffickers paint fairytales using deceit to trick their victims into trusting them and thinking they are falling in love, only to pull the rug out from under them by sexually exploiting them for profit. They aren't always pimps wearing fur coats and carrying canes, strutting around with feathers in their hats like in the movies, but instead might look like a tall, dark, handsome stud who knows how to treat his love interest with tender care and affection. And sometimes they look like weasels who can't get a girlfriend without targeting vulnerable young girls (who often have a difficult time separating truth from fiction when clouded by all of the layers of deception that these predators spew).

This romantic manipulation is the type of grooming and trafficking that the infamous Tate brothers have been accused of by Romanian authorities.[7] Sneaky Romeo Pimp traffickers know it can be nearly impossible for their victims to self-identify because they perceive they have a genuine relationship with the trafficker.

LIGHTBULB MOMENT

Traffickers practice mind-control techniques and use the power of persuasion to groom their victims, convincing them that they are making an empowered choice to be sold.

By using manufactured trust and manipulation, they trap their victims in a downward spiral and a web of lies. Their evil intent is always money-motivated, and they couldn't care less about the damage and destruction their victims experience.

As you'll read when I share my story, I was trafficked as a teen by men in their thirties. They pretended to be my boyfriends, and I thought they loved me. I was just a naive little girl looking for someone to love me. These men were already criminals who had done prison time and knew what it was like to live a lifestyle of criminal activity.

And they saw me as a goldmine.

With no protective father figure to guide and guard me, I had already been trafficked for ten years. My boundaries were nonexistent, I had low self-esteem, and I already had addictions that I needed to feed. These criminals targeted me, manipulated me into trusting them, and then they trafficked me for their own financial gain.

Social Media Manipulation

My trafficking and abuse started when I was a child, during the 1980's and 90's. This was pre-internet, so the traffickers had to come into contact with me on a one-on-one basis. Now we live in a much different time, and technological advances have given traffickers and predators several advantages. The digital world our children are growing up in makes it easier for traffickers to reach vulnerable targets and begin the grooming process.

A question that concerned parents often ask is, *How do groomers target kids on social media?*

The sad truth is traffickers don't have a very hard time finding ways to build trust with kids who are oversharing personal information online. This is how traffickers groom and exploit their victims, and today they have face-to-face access to vulnerable teens through the handheld devices our modern breakthroughs in technology provide.

Traffickers are targeting young kids, and they will often use online methods to groom those potential victims, shying away from risky snatch-and-grab methods that involve kidnapping children. Using the anonymity and intimacy created through private messaging, the trafficker can break down boundaries, build false trust, and present the illusion of being a kid.

Teens may not know how to ask for guidance about inappropriate messages or pictures they might receive on chat apps or situations they find themselves in through their social media connections. And they might be afraid they'll get in trouble for the unsolicited images they were sent, creating yet another stumbling block to seeking help to navigate the dangerous situation.

The manipulative ways traffickers use technology to groom and exploit children put them at a marked advantage over their young, naive targets. And traffickers know that parents are often out of touch with the latest communication channels, so they can have their way with little to no interference.

This is why I encourage parents to have age-appropriate conversations with their kids about the dangers they face every time they log onto a chat app, video game console, or social media site. Parents can keep open communication and build trust to make it easier for youngsters to confide in them when they face an inappropriate situation.

If you have a child in your life who discloses that illicit images are being requested or received, or shares any information about possible *targeting, grooming, or exploitation* online or "irl" (in real life), a virtual report can be made to NCMEC at https://report.cybertip.org/.[8] To report information about a missing or exploited child, call their 24-Hour Call Center: 1-800-THE-LOST (1-800-843-5678). If the child or someone they know is in immediate danger, please call 911 or your local police immediately.

Exposing the Industry of Exploitation

Trafficking is an economic play for those counting the cash. While traffickers act as recruiters, searching out vulnerable people they can manipulate into the illicit industry, the buyers keep the criminals in business by paying the price to access a person being marketed and sold as a product. In the next chapter, we will dig deeper into the twisted triangle traffickers use to turn people into products, producing profits.

Human traffickers see themselves as legitimate businesspeople. Traffickers use the same methods to establish, grow, and scale their businesses as upstanding professionals. It may be as simple as using the internet to advertise their "products" or to book a hotel room and rental car, or banking at a trusted financial institution and investing their profits.

But make no mistake, there is nothing beneficial to society about a person who would be willing to put a price tag on another human being. Once you know how to decipher the subtle signs that trafficking is occurring in your community, you'll be able to take action and do something to stop the predators from destroying more lives.

---

[1] Unites States Attorney's Office: Southern District of New York. "Ghislaine Maxwell Sentenced to 20 Years in Prison For Conspiring With Jeffrey Epstein to Sexually Abuse Minors," June 28, 2022, https://www.justice.gov/usao-sdny/pr/ghislaine-maxwell-sentenced-20-years-prison-conspiring-jeffrey-epstein-sexually-abuse.

[2] Cabral, Sam, "JP Morgan Agrees to Pay $290m to Settle Lawsuit Brought by Jeffrey Epstein Victims," BBC, June 12, 2023, https://www.bbc.com/news/world-us-canada-65879833.

[3] Skipworth, William, "JP Morgan Will Pay Virgin Islands $75 Million Settlement Over Jeffrey Epstein Lawsuit," Forbes, September 26, 2023, https://www.forbes.com/sites/willskipworth/2023/09/26/jpmorgan-will-pay-virgin-islands-75-million-settlement-over-jeffrey-epstein-lawsuit/.

[4] Neumeister, Larry, and Ken Sweet, "JPMorgan CEO Jamie Dimon Says He Never Heard of Jeffrey Epstein Until After His 2019 Arrest," AP News, May 31, 2023, https://apnews.com/article/jeffrey-epstein-jpmorgan-lawsuit-jamie-dimon-8f696fc69620dbc885cf6d5cb8a6cbfd.

[5] U.S. Department of Justice. "Human Trafficking Incidents Reported by Law Enforcement, 2022—Statistical Tables." December 2024. https://bjs.ojp.gov/document/htirle22st.pdf.

[6] Casassa, K., Ploss, A., & Karandikar, S., "'He Loves Me Hard and Then He Abuses Me Hard': How Service Providers Define and Explain Trauma Bonds Among Sex Trafficking Survivors." Sage Journals, Violence Against Women, February 16, 2023, https://doi.org/10.1177/10778012231158104.

[7] Eidell, Lynsey, "Who Are the Tate Brothers? What to Know About Disgraced Influencers Andrew and Tristan Tate and the Criminal Charges Against Them," People, March 20, 2025, https://people.com/tate-brothers-andrew-tristan-what-to-know-8611741.

[8] https://report.cybertip.org/

Chapter 3

THE INDUSTRY OF EXPLOITATION
Flesh for Sale—Business Is Booming

As a society, we may not be able to prevent every vulnerability from affecting the population—things like poverty, addiction, unstable living situations, mental illness, lack of social awareness, and the unfortunate vulnerability of youth—but by becoming educated in the ways traffickers operate, we can work to make it dangerous and unprofitable for the criminal who exploits the vulnerable and turns their victims into a product for profit.

Traffickers often network with other traffickers, and they usually work together to create an illicit marketplace. When law enforcement takes down a trafficker's business, the other traffickers who are in their networks feel the heat, especially as they see their former business associates being held to justice.

Dismantling these criminal networks is key to bringing an end to human trafficking. We can begin that process by understanding the three-sided structure of the Human Trafficking Triangle.

The Human Trafficking Triangle

In the economic triangle, three specific components must be at play for commerce to be established: First, a *product* must exist, then that product must be brought into the marketplace by a *supplier* who sells it to the customer, driving *demand.* If there is no one willing to pay for the product and the exchange of value does not happen, the product will not be sold.

When we inspect the economics of the Human Trafficking Triangle, we find there are three distinct components involved as well: A trafficker symbolizes the supplier (or merchant) who sells a product (the victim) to the buyer, who is driving demand in the marketplace. Unfortunately, in this example, the product is a precious human who was born with a purpose and promise, whose intrinsic value far supersedes any price tag placed on it.

In this twisted situation, the trafficker gets what he wants: money.

The buyer gets what he wants: sexual contact or cheap goods and services.

And the person being commodified ends up losing in the exploitative equation.

LIGHTBULB MOMENT

Human trafficking exists when an enterprising trafficker exploits a vulnerable person to make a profit from a willing buyer, and that profit lines the trafficker's pockets.

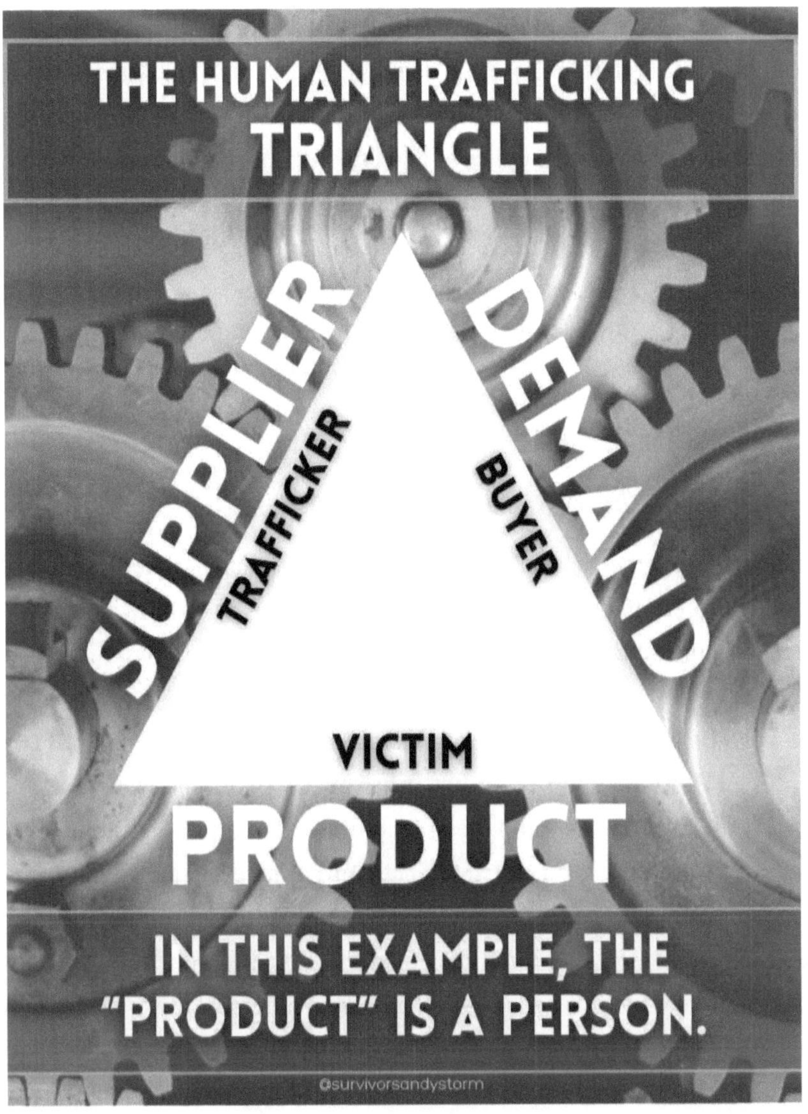

Human traffickers are opportunists, and they will manipulate anything to get an advantage in their criminal enterprise. These traffickers identify and exploit vulnerabilities so they can turn people into products that produce profits, and the more desperate a target is, the easier it will be to coerce that individual into forced labor or the industry of commercial sexual exploitation.

This crime creates an illicit black market where people are turned into products and purchasers drive the demand. The crime of human trafficking can exist within legitimate businesses, creating an outlet for the illegal trade of victims under the cover of legal operations. Let's break down each of the components in the Human Trafficking Triangle to see a clear picture of how this illicit marketplace functions. Once you're able to discern the way the traffickers and buyers rely on one another, you'll be able to see these dynamics at play as you read my story in the following chapters.

Traffickers: The Suppliers

Trafficking Is a Business, Not a Love Affair

Understanding the market drivers and systems that traffickers need to establish to produce profits in their illicit enterprise is key to identifying, dismantling, and dissolving trafficking networks in our communities.

The common theme running through every case of human trafficking is a person who has identified a vulnerability in another person's life and exploited that vulnerability for his or her own selfish, financial gain.

Traffickers act as marketers, and they dress their victims up in wrappers to put them out for sale. They might take victims shopping for designer clothes or spend money having their hair or nails done, justifying those expenses as part of their investment to put a high-end product on the market. When someone seeking to purchase a person looks at the outer packaging, they see a piece of merchandise designed to fulfill their desires, whether for sexual servitude or another form of indentured bondage to the financial exchange.

These traffickers and buyers use the same tools and technology that other legitimate businesses use to create profits. They might advertise online, using websites and social media to put their product line on a virtual shelf. Traffickers also commonly use cell phone technology and chat apps to communicate with buyers and coordinate drop-off, pickup, and payment exchange. The same cash exchange or credit card processing tools used by honest businesspeople are exploited by traffickers to collect their profits. Legal business owners buy plane tickets, rent cars, and stay in hotels or Airbnbs when they travel. Similarly, within their criminal enterprises, traffickers organize business trips using those same transportation modes and travel plans.

LIGHTBULB MOMENT

 **Human trafficking defies borders, and it doesn't care what side of the tracks someone is from.**

While we have built an understanding of some types of circumstances traffickers find appealing in a victim, it's important to understand that there is no perfect victim profile with only one certain background. No segment of society is immune. Some traffickers seek people in poverty and use the lure of money to trap them in cycles of exploitation, while other traffickers seek victims from more affluent communities so they can market them to high-class buyers who expect the people they are paying for to be educated and understand the etiquette of polite society.

Endless Vulnerabilities Create Endless Opportunities for Traffickers

What vulnerabilities do traffickers look for in their potential victims?

Unfortunately, the list is virtually endless. Young people like children and teens have innumerable vulnerabilities that traffickers will exploit to gain a position of trust. They will stop at nothing to groom a vulnerable child into the world of exploitation. Traffickers are aware of the possibility that the guilt and shame that young victims experience might prevent them from seeing the reality of their situation. This means victims will become compliant with their exploitation and remain trapped in the cycles of abuse instead of attempting to escape.

Trafficking occurs in every community worldwide across a diverse assortment of cultures, but there are common vulnerabilities that precipitate trafficking that do remain consistent worldwide. For example, there are networks of power players on every level of society who seek to leverage the desperation of a parent as a way to gain access to a child.

Familial Trafficking and Empty Promises of Love

Why would a parent put his or her own child in the marketplace?

What level of poverty or desperation could persuade a mother to allow her vulnerable child to be commodified to obtain resources? How could a father use his kid as a transaction, no matter how displaced, homeless, addicted, or otherwise unstable he is?

In his book *Sex Trafficking: Inside the Business of Modern Slavery*, Harvard researcher and Frederick Douglass Book Prize winner Siddharth Kara[1] visited the darkest corners of the earth to seek answers to these questions. What he discovered and exposed is far more sinister than the heart can bear.

Money and status are used to put people into situations that they don't see another way out of; the parent receives a false sense of security or provision, the exploiter receives a fleeting moment of pleasure, and the child lives with compounded trauma—sometimes living in a continuous cycle of trauma, addiction, and desperation as a result of the experience.

> The same conditions of poverty, desperation, and displacement lead many families to sell a child into slavery.[2]

As Kara looks at the global sex trade and pulls back the curtain on how this crime is affecting people around the world, he notes, "Many victims of forced prostitution are originally acquired through promises of love."

Traffickers don't always look like villains. As I've experienced, sometimes a trafficker comes in the form of a friend, family member, or loving partner. Disguising themselves in this way increases their odds of success, as their victims are likely to trust them from the start.

Other Forms of Trafficking

Human trafficking is not limited to commercial sexual exploitation but is modern slavery in any form, and it impacts every segment of our society. Enterprising traffickers are exploiting supply chains in many legitimate businesses so they can turn a profit through their illicit practices.

Cobalt Red, another compelling book by Siddharth Kara, exposes the abhorrent exploitation of entire communities, the raping of the land in the Congo, and the blatant disregard for the sanctity of human life that keeps the mad dash churning for this precious mineral—cobalt.

After reading *Cobalt Red*, I will never look at plugging in a phone, laptop, car, or any other rechargeable battery the same way again. Children have died tunneling underground and digging in toxic dirt piles, hunting for cobalt so they can earn less than $1 a day, just so I can have a rechargeable tech device worth more than they will earn in their entire lifetimes. The important information in this groundbreaking book can help create true change as more people become aware of the exploitation that is rampant in the rechargeable battery industry.

Closer to home, the U.S. State Department has released its annual "Trafficking in Persons Report" (also referred to as the TIP Report) each year since 2001.[3] The 2024 TIP Report spotlights the impact of digital technology in the trafficking arena and places a special interest on organ trafficking and the exploitation of persons with disabilities.

By analyzing global law enforcement data, highlighting work with partners throughout the world to implement a prevention protocol, and recognizing heroes in the work to address the issue of trafficking worldwide, this report includes a list of some of the industries where victims of forced labor have been exploited. From restaurants to retail, even big businesses we rely on each day for technology and transportation are afflicted by this problem of labor trafficking.

Some settings the TIP Report identifies as hot spots for trafficking include:

- Agricultural fields
- Factories
- Restaurants
- Hotels
- Massage parlors
- Retail stores
- Fishing vessels
- Mines
- Private homes
- Drug trafficking operations

While certain types of human trafficking may be more prevalent in other countries (such as organ trafficking, forced marriages, and child labor), trafficking does happen here in the United States, both to Americans and by Americans.

Buyers: The Demand

Depravity-Driven Demand

As you will read in the chapters ahead, there seemed to be a never-ending supply of men who were willing to take advantage of me in my weakest moments. At the end of the day, they got what they wanted, and I paid the price. None of those men were ever held accountable for their abhorrent actions, so we will never know how many others they purchased and later tossed aside.

Perhaps even more disturbing is the fact that there is still an active and growing demand for the sale of vulnerable young people to fulfill the deviant sexual urges of financially affluent buyers. These buyers flood the market, creating a demand that can be met by enterprising traffickers who hawk the flesh of children and teens for a hefty profit. This demand drives the traffickers to *target, groom, and exploit* young victims so they can create income.

Like traffickers and victims, sex buyers can come from any walk of life, culture, race, or religion, but they all have one thing in common—they see the human *body as a commodity* to be consumed. The trafficker capitalizes on the buyer's porn-sick desires and serves the victim on a platter to the highest bidder.

The sad truth is that the inhumane industry of commercial sexual exploitation traps both the buyer and the victim in a deceitful web of oppressive behavior and injustice. Buying and selling people will never be a victimless crime. Traffickers don't care what buyers do to their "product" so long as they pay the fee. There is abundant evidence that buyers are abusive and degrade the people they purchase, feeling as if they have a right to do whatever they want because they forked over cash to buy that person for the hour or night.

The twisted culture that drives the demand for sex-for-sale directly feeds the human trafficking market. The buyers are primarily men who see bodies as commodities, and they're looking for a victim who is willing to do anything for money, even if it's their only means of survival.

While it might be easier to see the person being sold as a victim who has been violated, the buyers are often caught in destructive cycles that lead them down devastating pathways of destruction, all for the benefit of the trafficker who safely sits on the sidelines, counting the cash collected by destroying lives.

Whether they justify their self-serving actions or simply act as entitled consumers, there is no denying that the men driving the demand for trafficked individuals are a black mark on society. The abusive behavior they display toward trafficking victims leaves scars on the souls of those being bought.

LIGHTBULB MOMENT

 **Participating in the industry of commercial sexual exploitation directly feeds into the human trafficking market, whether through street prostitution, brothels, escort services, online pornography, or any other way humans are bought and sold.**

If we are going to curb demand, we must educate men about how being involved in the buying side of the sex industry is damaging to their own souls and psyches, as well as to the person being purchased. A plethora of research on the destructive ways the consumption of pornography and participating in prostitution is harming society and destroying lives can be found at Dr. Gail Dine's culturereframed.org; Dr. Melissa Farley's prostitutionresearch.com; and through the Demand Forum presented by the National Center on Sexual Exploitation (NCOSE) at demand-forum.org.

Money Can't Buy You Love

Money can only buy an illusion of intimacy. Paying for sex is renting a body to use and abuse for selfish, greedy purposes. The transaction can never fulfill the desire for intimacy and oneness that a consensual encounter brings. Instead, these experiences leave both participants even emptier than before.

According to research from Demand Abolition, as many as 16% of men are active sex purchasers, 99% of sex buyers are men, and as many as one in five men have rented the body of another human being at least once in their lifetime.[4]

If these stats are even close to accurate, we need to start discussing the truth about trafficking with the men in our lives. These crucial conversations can educate and empower men to act as heroes instead of predators.

This isn't an attack on every Tom, Dick, and Harry, but it is a clarion call to men to hold one another accountable to treat everyone with dignity, honor, and respect. If men were not driving the demand, sex traffickers would not be able to make a profit from exploiting vulnerable individuals.

Exploitation can indeed affect anyone, but the most typical gender dynamics of a sex trafficking situation involve a female (or feminine/submissive) victim and a dominating male buyer. The entire sex industry has been established and built upon gender-based violence and crime against women and children.

Going to strip clubs and watching pornography are damaging behaviors to society. These indulgences make it dangerous for vulnerable people to exist in society. At some point, people who are driving the demand for the weak to be exploited need to ask themselves, "Is this really the world I want to live in?" and, "Is this really the world I want to raise my kids in?"

Scientific evidence of the harmful ways pornography rewires the brain is documented in Gary Wilson's book *Your Brain on Porn*. Pornography usage has been shown to lead to sexual dysfunction, anxiety, cognitive disorders, and compulsive addictive behaviors. To discover more about the ways the porn industry is linked to sex trafficking and how to break free from digital addiction, free resources are available from the nonprofit Fight the New Drug at fightthenewdrug.org.

In the industry of commercial sexual exploitation, it is easy to see that most of the buyers are male, and these men are often married with families and have jobs that provide them with the discretionary income they use to buy and rent "disposable" people. Even more disturbing is the sad truth that these men behind the demand are often community leaders or hold a position of respect and authority. Continually being bought and abused by people who should be protecting them can make it even more difficult for victims to break the destructive cycle.

When a trafficker wants to grow his supply, he will look for vulnerable people he can control and manipulate. But no matter how much he degrades and abuses his victims, he will never make any money unless a buyer is representing the market demand. This is precisely why we need to work towards an end to the demand that is driving the industry of commercial sexual exploitation and any other areas where trafficking is prevalent.

Demand Drivers Tied to Your Spending Decisions

The drivers propelling the demand are revealed for other types of human trafficking when we look critically at the market. For example, budget-conscious buyers seeking low prices on household goods may not realize that one of the ways the supplier was able to pass on savings was by using forced labor to produce the product. Or, a tech-savvy shopper who wants the latest, cutting-edge device might not be aware that trafficking victims were exploited to mine the minerals used in their rechargeable batteries.

Consumers are often surprised to learn that some items and industries that have historically been rife with exploitation and trafficking include chocolate, coffee, sugar, fast fashion, and precious metals and stones. Children and other vulnerable people are known to be used as slaves to pick blueberries, spin thread, mine metals, and more.

As responsible, educated, compassionate citizens, we have the opportunity to make choices about our purchases based on the overall benefit to society, not on the dollar amount we will save on the sale. We can raise the standards in the marketplace by researching the companies we do business with and sharing our anti-slavery values with the businesses we buy from. Once we find reputable suppliers of our favorite goods and services, we can share the information about these companies with our friends and families, encouraging them to shop slave-free as well.

The more we drive market demand for fair-trade products, the more suppliers will either step up to act responsibly, or they will go out of business because their unethical practices are exposed. Our dollars can push companies to keep supply chains transparent and hold businesses accountable to treating their employees and contractors with dignity by paying them fair wages.

When we consider the devastating impact made on a victim who has been bought and sold as a slave, it becomes easier to make choices to reject pornography and strip clubs or seek fair-trade goods and slave-free industries. Pushing for an end to the demand is a key to seeing trafficking come to an end.

Victims: The Product

Creating Walking Money Machines

Traffickers are focused on one thing only—making money. They don't care who gets preyed upon or at what cost.

Traffickers are playing both sides of the game, and both the victim and the buyer are being manipulated and exploited. They capitalize on the buyer's porn-sick or penny-pinching desires and serve the victims to them on demand. I am not saying that these buyers are innocent by any means, but I do want to expose the corrupt ways traffickers engage in illicit business practices at the expense of both victim and buyer.

A trafficker is more likely someone who has worked hard to build credibility and trust so they have access to be alone with a young person. These exploiters look for every opportunity they can find to turn a vulnerable child into a walking ATM.

LIGHTBULB MOMENT

The truth of human trafficking doesn't look like a fast-paced Hollywood action movie but more like a dirty alleyway, a filthy motel room, or a haunting street corner.

Traffickers don't discriminate, and buyers don't care if they're in a rickety, run-down shack or a high-class, five-star resort. These people only care about getting what they want. Traffickers only want money, and they don't care about who gets hurt in their pursuit. Sex buyers only want a body to use to fulfill their selfish, carnal desires, and they don't care about the damage their choices leave on others.

When a trafficker wants cash, they simply send out their victims with a quota to meet before the night is over, turning their victims into currency dispensers. Traffickers then use that money to rent hotel rooms, eat and drink at restaurants and bars, go on shopping sprees, or buy tickets for expensive concerts or sporting events. They buy luxurious cars, houses, electronics, and designer clothing at the expense of their victims' exploitation.

It can be easy to miss the signs of trafficking because the victims are so often hidden in plain sight. But traffickers and buyers aren't the only ones contributing to the problem of human trafficking. Society's looking the other way also keeps the victims trapped in the illicit world of the industry of commercial sexual exploitation.

Human trafficking degrades the entire community, attracting bad actors and enabling criminal networks to expand the scope of their crimes. How has our world spun so out of control that we now live in a culture that makes it easy for a little girl to lose her innocence and a little boy to become an exploiter?

LIGHTBULB MOMENT

No child dreams of having her body sold to strangers, and no child dreams of treating his fellow human being as a product.

Disposable People are Easily Replaced

The National Center for Missing and Exploited Children (NCMEC) is one of the few organizations that compiles reliable data that we can use to objectively look into the problem of domestic minor sex trafficking and commercial sexual exploitation of children. They have data showing that children around fifteen years old are often sought out by enterprising traffickers, and they are put on the black market to be sold to voracious buyers who want younger and younger victims.

Traffickers see their victims as disposable. Once they get the money out of them, they discard the victim without a second thought. Victims of trafficking might seem to vanish into thin air. These are daughters and sons, neighbors, students, friends, and members of our communities who cannot be replaced. Each one is valuable—a person created with dignity and purpose. Unfortunately, many of the missing and exploited children NCMEC is helping law enforcement search for may be victims of trafficking.

With traffickers motivated to target a victim who will be quickly and easily groomed and exploited, they often look to the hundreds of thousands of children involved in the foster care system within the U.S. The traffickers know foster kids may have already experienced a life of abuse, neglect, and assault. Another benefit to a trafficker is the lower likelihood that the victim will have a parent or guardian overly involved in her life. This makes the foster care system a fertile hunting ground for traffickers seeking vulnerable victims. Once they get what they want from their victims—money—they toss them aside and set out in search of another person they can turn a profit through.

I spent a short time in the foster system when I was just 12 years old. During that period, it was nearly impossible to find someone I could trust who wasn't taking advantage of me. While I wasn't yet a teenager, I had already been abused by my parents for years. I never had any examples of people who had made a proper life for themselves.

I'm grateful that I survived these situations that so many others don't find an escape from. Unfortunately, I know of others who were trapped in trafficking situations like me, and they never found freedom; they died while still being exploited. The traffickers saw them as disposable and replaceable. The illicit trafficking enterprise has continued churning, and today, it is bigger and stronger than ever before.

Drug addiction and alcohol dependence are powerful tools for traffickers. People struggling with addictions can be more vulnerable to traffickers because they're already involved in a criminal world where they search out suppliers, but the trafficker can also leverage the addiction to maintain control over that victim.

Traffickers want compliant victims who will do as instructed without putting up a fight, and they often dangle a carrot in front of their victims to coax them to continue turning profits. That drug could come in the form of an addictive substance or the target's drug of choice.

Because of the societal stigma of addiction, traffickers can count on their victims being overlooked. When they want to dispose of a victim who is not bringing in enough cash or is starting to put up resistance, it is thought to be a common practice for traffickers to use a "hot shot"[5] that can look like an accidental overdose to a homicide detective.

A Word of Warning and Wisdom

It is important to always keep in mind that human trafficking is a crime, and traffickers are criminals who can become aggressive or unpredictable when confronted. They not only have their profits to protect, but they might be motivated to react violently to confrontation because the laws they are breaking could result in hefty punishments, including imprisonment, fines, and being listed on the sex offender registry. Understanding the motives and market drivers behind the illicit human trafficking market can help expose illegal operations at work within our communities, but we should never try to take the law into our own hands.

LIGHTBULB MOMENT

A well-meaning citizen should never approach a suspected trafficker or attempt to rescue a suspected victim.

Contrary to popular belief, rescuing victims is not the solution to ending human trafficking. It's always a reason to rejoice if someone breaks free from the horrific abuses they have suffered at the hands of a human trafficker, but the exploitation will continue with another victim unless the exploiter is stopped.

When a victim is removed from a trafficker's control, that trafficker is incentivized to replace the victim with another money-making "product." Without the trafficker being taken out of the equation, the number of victims will increase each time someone is rescued, so involving law enforcement and allowing them to build a prosecutable case is of the highest importance.

Unless you are a trained law enforcement officer, you should never attempt to intervene directly in a suspected trafficking situation. The uncertainty and unpredictability of the circumstances, along with the possibility that the trafficker could have weapons or be involved with other illegal activity (like firearms or narcotics trafficking), make this a highly unsafe situation for an untrained person to navigate.

Shows like *COPS, Takedown, To Catch a Predator* with Chris Hansen, or *America's Most Wanted* with John Walsh give us a glimpse into the minds of alleged criminals who desire to hurt vulnerable people, like a child who is being sold online. When they are caught, these accused criminals often try to use psychologically manipulative techniques to solicit sympathy and compassion from the arresting officers and anyone else they can persuade to hear their defense.

Many people and organizations within the anti-trafficking space claim they enact justice, but if the criminal exploiters who buy and sell trafficking victims aren't prosecuted, they will find more vulnerable people to exploit. The sad truth is that vigilantes and rogue organizations do more harm than good because they often interfere with true justice being established. We have to keep our communities safe from these criminals by enforcing laws that hold the offenders accountable.

The only person who can properly apprehend a trafficker and recover a victim is a trained law enforcement officer. Even the most well-intentioned citizen trying to intervene could interfere with an ongoing investigation or find themselves in a dangerous circumstance. Without the law being upheld and enforced, the trafficker will never be held accountable for their crimes, and there will never be true justice for the victims.

If you suspect you have information about human trafficking, the best course of action is always to call local law enforcement and make a report. Take care to include as much information as possible—location and time of day, physical descriptors, and details about what you witnessed, including clothing descriptions, license plate numbers, or make and model of any vehicles involved. If the situation involves a suspected minor, an act of physical violence, or any other dire circumstance, calling 911 is highly recommended for a faster response.

Reporting to law enforcement might seem intimidating, but if desired, you can always remain anonymous. And you can be encouraged that your tip might be the missing link to bring a trafficker to justice and set his victims free.

During the decades I was a victim of human trafficking, I thought everyone was conspiring against me. As a six year old child, the people who were meant to care for and protect me violated and abused me. As a teen, I found it especially difficult to see police officers and authority figures as trustworthy since I had been part of a criminal underground and was deeply addicted to illegal drugs. My traffickers often manipulated situations so they could gain empathy and support, leaving me confused and unable to pursue justice. This discouraged me from seeking assistance to escape my situation and prosecute my traffickers. I needed an advocate to fight for me.

When I think of the twenty years when I was being trafficked, I remember countless incidents over that time when someone saw something they could have reported to law enforcement. With the right tip from a concerned citizen, a police officer could have helped me escape the abuse and exploitation I was suffering through each day. But, because no one understood the situation I was in, instead of freeing me from the traffickers who were exploiting me, each encounter I had with authority drove me deeper into the darkness and despair.

The next section of this book is my true story of surviving twenty years as a victim of pedophiles and human traffickers. Remember the trigger warning, and try some of the recommended self-care practices if you become distraught while unpacking this story. Hold onto hope because you know, despite all the horrific experiences, *I survived,* and I'm living a healthy and blessed life today.

As you read the details of the events I endured, remember to watch for glimpses of how the TRUTH about human trafficking was hidden in plain sight.

---

[1] Kara is one of the few researchers who have brought solid data out of the field and documented thousands of cases of slavery. Much of his work is driven solely by his passion to uncover the truth and is largely self-funded. A champion in the fight to end human trafficking, Kara has brought together his unwavering search for the truth, partnered with his ability to treat each human he encounters with honor and dignity to give us honest looks into trafficking throughout the world. His work can help us understand the global economic impact of trafficking.

[2] Kara, Siddharth, *Sex Trafficking: Inside the Business of Modern Slavery.* Columbia University Press, 2017. https://doi.org/10.7312/kara18033.

[3] U.S. Department of State. "Trafficking in Persons Report." https://www.state.gov/wp-content/uploads/2025/02/TIP-Report-2024_Introduction_V10_508-accessible_2.13.2025.pdf.

[4] Demand Abolition. "Facts About Men Who Buy Sex." Research. January 2016. https://www.demandabolition.org/research/.

[5] "What Is a Hot Shot of Heroin?" https://sunshinebehavioralhealth.com/opioid/heroin/what-is-a-hot-shot-of-heroin/ September 26, 2025.

PART TWO

My Story of Survival

Chapter 4

THE PEDOPHILE RING: CHILD TRAFFICKING IN AMERICA
Sold in Suburbia

6-12 years old

Child sex trafficking is real.
Pedophile rings are real.
Parents selling their daughters and sons are real.
This is not a conspiracy theory. I lived it, and I survived.

Growing up in the 1980s, when I was a victim of the crimes of familial trafficking and sexual abuse, I witnessed many other children trapped in the same living hell as I was. It probably doesn't look like what you think it does, but child trafficking is a sad reality in the U.S. and around the globe. Vulnerable children are prime targets for traffickers because they are easily groomed and manipulated.

Today, I boldly share the truth about trafficking so we can bring an end to this evil, set the captives free, and see traffickers receive the justice they deserve. The information you read in the next few chapters might be difficult to process, and my intent is not to be graphic or triggering but to share the reality of my experience with clarity to equip you with the information you need to bring an end to human trafficking for those still trapped in the exploitation.

As I describe some of the situations I lived through, take note of how you can see the patterns of grooming and exploitation to identify the TRUTH about trafficking throughout my story.

Building a Tolerance for Trauma

When I look back at my childhood, I see that the vulnerabilities exploited by nefarious traffickers had emerged many years before I was trafficked. These unprotected blind spots were identified by the traffickers and used to their advantage when I was just a six-year-old kindergartener. But the abuse, dysfunction, and exploitation had started years before that.

Growing up in the small midwestern town of Clayton, my mother was the oldest of six children. Her dad, my grandpa, worked at a nearby factory for a meager income, but he struggled to keep food on the table. Exposure to poverty and lack—and likely her own story of neglect and abuse—led my mother to drugs, alcohol, and desperation.

My parents met when my mother was a junior at Clayton High School, and she dropped out so they could get married. She wanted my father to be her savior and help her escape from her impoverished circumstances, but he struggled with mental illness and soon became physically abusive. He was violent and unpredictable, and when he would stop taking his medication, he would hallucinate due to his unmanaged schizophrenia.

Soon after they wed, I was born into poverty, as the firstborn child brought into a family already swirling with violence, addiction, and mental illness. Tragedy struck when I was just five years old; my father died by suicide, leaving my mother a widow and my younger sister and me orphans. We didn't have much money, and my mother started looking for another man to fill the gaps and allow her to live a higher quality of life.

She met the man she was looking for at a small convenience and liquor store at the edge of town. Mr. Earl's parents owned the store, and he called himself a businessman. My mother was impressed by his tales of traveling and his offer to build her a new life in a city far away. He convinced her that they could buy a new house and live according to their own rules. Mr. Earl promised to get her a new car and nice clothes, and he told her that my sister and I would have all the toys we could ever want and go to good schools in a wealthy part of town.

Mr. Earl soon rented the house directly across the street from my grandparents and moved my mother, sister, and me in. Not long after we moved, he called me into his bedroom one afternoon, right after he had taken a shower. My mother and little sister were watching cartoons in the living room, but I went into his bedroom where he and my mother slept. I still remember the way the scent of his shampoo filled the space.

That is the first time I remember him abusing me, but it did not seem abusive. It felt like a special time when I was able to do something with him that earned me a lot of praise. He told me what good girls and pretty ladies like to do to men, and when I did as I was instructed, he heaped compliments upon me, telling me I had made him very, very happy.

When I came out of the bedroom to go back to the living room to play with my baby dolls and watch cartoons, my mother was jealous and acted cold and angry towards me. It was confusing and difficult for my six-year-old mind to understand, but I quickly learned that doing what my new stepdad wanted me to do earned me special treats and lots of positive attention from him. I also discovered how to gain that positive praise from other men and women that he introduced me to as I got older.

After a short time, Mr. Earl moved us to another house about a mile away from my grandparents' place. When we relocated to that new house, my stepdad gave me a plush stuffed animal—a purple unicorn with a golden horn. He told me every time I looked at my new toy, he wanted me to think of his "horn." He said he was the only "horn" for me.

During that time, there were many days when I would be alone with my stepdad, and he always wanted to make me comfortable with being nude with him, so we sometimes took showers together. This behavior and sexual abuse happened daily, and it was all normalized to me. This was part of the grooming and conditioning process.

As my kindergarten school year came to a close, my stepdad convinced my mother to move away from Clayton and start the new life they had been dreaming of. That summer, we packed up what little we had and drove across the country to a city 1,500 miles away from the watchful eyes of the family and nosy neighbors in our small community.

A Whole New Way of Life

Arriving in the new place was like a dream coming true. This city was built on the Gulf Coast, and the downtown area hugged a sparkling bay that created a beautiful backdrop where high-rise condos and office buildings overlooked a waterfront full of sailboats and seagulls. We were in a subtropical paradise complete with swaying palm trees, a sandy seashore, and beautiful beach houses. This was an incredible opportunity, especially considering the life of poverty we had left behind in Clayton.

It was like we had hit the jackpot, but things weren't at all as good as they seemed. The truth was that we were homeless and didn't have many resources to get started. The business Mr. Earl was involved in had not yet generated any money, but it did not take long for things to change.

When we first arrived in the Gulf Coast city, we had to camp in a tent on the beach while we waited for an apartment to open up for us to move into. We used public showers at the beach where we inserted quarters to release the lukewarm spray that would wash away the salt and sand. After showering and putting on clean clothes, I was taken to school for my first-grade class. It might be surprising, but I attended school just like all the other kids, and I excelled in my classes because I was always eager to gain the approval and praise of adults.

After school, I came back to the tent with Mr. Earl and my mother. Sometimes they took me to an all-nude beach where men and women were looking for children to condition and abuse. I was a tiny six-year-old girl, and these adults were training me to be a compliant, submissive, obedient slave. My new stepdad was a pedophile, and he took advantage of any opportunity he could to groom me. This man and my mother had insatiable appetites for perversion, and as an innocent little girl who craved praise from the adults in my life, I was the perfect victim.

Because I wanted to be a good girl and show obedience to the adults who were investing so much time, energy, and attention into indoctrinating me, I fulfilled every sick, twisted desire of the man who was violating me daily. His abuse did not seem abusive to me, but it was instead like the attention of a father figure who told me I was making him happy. Mr. Earl made molestation into my daily routine, and I had no frame of reference to understand that what he was doing was wrong. My body betrayed me by accepting and eventually craving his physical attention. And he introduced me to other abusive adults who repeatedly validated my obedience with praise.

I was isolated from any safe people, and these pedophiles turned my everyday reality into an exploration of sexuality and submission. They used any opportunity they could find to sexualize and desensitize me to nudity, pornography, and abuse. Exposure to graphic magazines, VHS tapes, and photos taught me how to perform and normalize these otherwise taboo behaviors.

Conditioning and Desensitization

Shortly after we arrived on the Gulf Coast, we were able to move out of the tent on the beach and into an apartment that overlooked the sparkling bay. Many of the people in our apartment complex drove nice vehicles and wore name-brand clothes. I wonder if any of the parents suspected the type of abuse I was experiencing daily behind the closed door of our apartment.

LIGHTBULB MOMENT

 **When concerned citizens learn the TRUTH about trafficking, they will be equipped to identify the subtle signs that traffickers display, make a report to law enforcement, and be part of the victim's freedom story.**

As a businessman, Mr. Earl was made the vice president of a department in a bank. He also held a license with the state as a commercial realtor, and even in the 1980s, he was often able to work from home and had his days free to network and meet with clients, associates, and friends. His bank connections gave him access to some of the repossessed items they had taken from debtors, and sometimes he would drive home in a Cadillac or a Lincoln Town Car. He may have appeared as an upstanding, successful businessman, but in reality, he was a devious criminal who was involved in a ring of pedophiles. These adults were sexually abusing children daily.

My mother often left me at the apartment all night with Mr. Earl and their growing collection of VHS pornography. Those videos acted as my training school, and I learned from the age of six years old that men like Mr. Earl and his friends wanted me to use my body to get rewards from them.

Children usually have a favorite movie they like watching, like a funny cartoon or a fantasy movie about dragons, princesses, and knights in shining armor. My favorite videotapes had a beautiful blonde lady on the covers. She was from Sweden, and to my childish mind, she was like a princess. I loved watching the men and women in the movies shower her with attention and bring her pleasure. I liked this actress so much that at six years old, when I received a little blonde baby doll for Christmas, I named it after her.

Many adults in my life commented that I was mature for my age and complimented my intelligence and manners. The adults who were abusing me used the flattering remarks as a way to condition me to receive praise from them for doing as instructed. At school, I was known as a teacher's pet, and I accelerated in my studies, being recognized as a promising student with potential. This placed me in smaller groups with even more one-on-one engagement with adults, which helped me to thrive. School was the only place where adults engaged with me without innuendo or sexualized contact.

Because they were able to interact and engage with me in a more personal and familiar way, if some of these upstanding, safe adults from my school had known the signs to look for, they may have been able to identify me as a victim of abuse. But I was so good at playing the part of an obedient child that it was not easy for them to see the subtle signals I displayed.

When I wasn't at school, I spent a lot of time with Mr. Earl and his friends, and they often told me I was pretty or teased me about being my "boyfriend." Most of the adult attention I received in my home or the places Mr. Earl took me was centered around sexual behaviors such as kissing and touching. It was common for adults to have me sit on their laps, as they groomed me to be open and receptive to their advances. I displayed signs that acted as signals to the abusers that I had been broken and conditioned.

Because of the daily abuse, my memories of baby dolls, cartoons, reading with my parents, movie nights, house parties, spending the night with friends, arts and crafts projects, days at the beach, and even Christmas and other defining childhood moments were all tainted with stains of sexualization and abuse.

LIGHTBULB MOMENT

When children are exposed to pornographic material, their view of reality is altered, and a filter of sexualization is applied to their world.

Country Clubs, Yacht Clubs, and Waterfront Homes

After a couple of years, it was time to move from the apartment complex, and the brand-new house my stepdad chose for us was on the same street as the recently constructed junior high school. The neighborhood was full of families, and the children walked to their classes at one of the school buildings on the sprawling campus. This was one of the highest-rated schools in the state, and I excelled in the TAG program for talented and gifted students.

My mother picked the colors of carpet and paint for our new home, and we had brand-new furniture delivered. Her favorite part of the house was the stone fireplace in the living room. She filled the cabinets in the kitchen with nice dishes and expensive cookware. We had a garage big enough to park two cars, but they usually left the Cadillac in the driveway as a way of showing off to the neighbors. They also had a van with curtains on the windows for privacy, and it had been custom-built with carpet on the walls and a sleeping area in the back.

Mr. Earl's professional positions allowed him access to country clubs and yacht clubs. There were several occasions when I was abused at places like these. One afternoon, I was taken to a country club and sent into a locker room with a man. He led me through the locker room and past the bathroom stalls and urinals, past the showers, and into a hidden room with leather couches and chairs. The feeling in the place was dark and sinister, but the man was not harsh or unkind to me. Instead, he praised me and said he would try to be gentle while he abused me.

One country club I was taken to had a sparkling pool, and I loved swimming with the other children and sunbathing in the "itsy bitsy, teeny weeny, yellow polka dot bikini" my mother gave me. I always received lots of compliments on my bathing suit from Mr. Earl and his friends. At this club, when I was sent to the locker room, a man was being unkind to a little girl I had been playing with in the pool. I froze and became uncompliant with the man who was attempting to coax me to perform for him. I got in trouble that day, and Mr. Earl was angry and stern with me on the drive home.

I also remember being taken to parties at a house with a sailboat on the dock. The house was big and fancy, filled with beautiful furniture and decorations. At one particular party, I was shown to a room upstairs, furnished with a big bed and a television. I was told to get comfy as the host switched on my favorite cartoons.

Not long after, a man came in with some cookies for me. After I ate the treats, he had me do things that made him happy, but when he finished abusing me, he cried and told me he was sorry before he left the room. Not long after, another man came in, and he lay down with me, telling me how pretty I was and stroking my hair. This same man would sometimes be on the sailboat when we would go out to the deep blue water, and he had a little bedroom inside the boat where he would abuse me.

Most of these experiences left me feeling like I was being a good girl, and I was often rewarded and praised for my obedience. This did not seem like abuse or assault because many of the people involved complimented me and gave me gifts. And because daily life in my home included being shown pornography and being molested by my stepdad, it became normal for me to engage in sexual activity with adults.

Mr. Earl was training me to be compliant. Like a puppy being disciplined, I was given treats and told that I was a "good girl" when I was obedient, and I was corrected or punished when I did something wrong. He used this grooming technique at all times, not just when he was abusing me. This was the way of life for every day of my childhood.

The sexual abuse and grooming continued nearly every day for six years. Mr. Earl used pornography and alcohol to teach me what to do and make me comfortable with his advances. By the time other men started coming to our upper-middle-class suburban home, I was familiar with how to perform. Whether I was taken to fancy parties at country clubs or to big houses along the water, I knew what was expected of me.

Mr. Earl and my mother were trafficking me for a better life. I was only a kid, and I never saw money exchange hands, but when we were with my stepdad, we weren't in poverty. The more people involved in the sexual abuse I was experiencing, the nicer cars we would drive, the bigger houses we would live in, and the more access we would have to country clubs, yacht clubs, and parties. This was a network of pedophiles who used pornography and child sexual abuse material to groom and traffic children like me.

I now see there was a cycle. They were all part of a network.

It was trafficking.

Progression into Perversion

My mother worked at a strip club and didn't spend much time at home. Sometimes I would ride with my stepdad to drop my mother off at work, and there was a big neon sign of a nearly naked, sexy woman in front of the building.

Once we got home from dropping my mother off, I would join Mr. Earl in the living room. He would have me make him a drink with the whiskey from the bar and ice out of the trays in the kitchen. Sometimes he would have me make myself a drink with sweet, fruity juice and one of the clear liquors in the bar. He would send me to the closet of the room he shared with my mother, where he would tell me to put on some of her clothes and pick out a VHS tape. The videos were on the top shelf, and I had to use a stool to reach them.

When I returned to the living room wearing my mother's clothes from her job at the strip club, I handed the videotape to my stepdad. He was always happy about the outfits and videos I chose, and he expressed his approval by showering me with compliments and positive attention. Sometimes the fruity drinks made me dizzy, making it easier for him to abuse me.

Mr. Earl had a dark-haired friend named Steve who visited us at our house, and at first, Steve would just come over to watch movies with us. Mr. Earl had me make them both whiskey drinks. Steve asked me lots of questions about what I liked about the movies and told me how much he liked my drinks.

One time when I was around ten years old, Steve brought a funny little cigarette that he smoked with me in the yard along the side of our house. After we puffed on the stinky joint, I got very dizzy and felt funny, and he asked me if I liked him. Giggling, I told him I thought he was cute, like the men in the videos, and he undid his pants so he could abuse me. Afterward, Steve left quickly, and Mr. Earl scolded me. He was upset because he didn't want sexual things to be done outside in the backyard.

Mr. Earl and Steve sometimes took pictures of me in my mother's clothes and set up a big movie camera in the living room. They showed me pictures or videos of other little girls like me doing things with grown-ups, and they instructed me to imitate the things I saw. Sometimes I drank fruity drinks or smoked one of the funny cigarettes with Steve. That helped me to do better at copying the movies or photos they showed me, which meant they were pleased with me. These experiences marked me and made it easy for the predators I encountered later in life, who knew what subtle signs to look for, to quickly identify me as a compliant, trained victim who would easily submit to their grooming and perversion.

The abuse I experienced did not look like what people probably think of when they consider the ways predators abuse children. I was treated with what I perceived as love and care. My mother had disciplined me to associate the sexual desire that these adults had for me as a good thing I should strive for. I had been trained to exude sexual energy and be cooperative and obedient to the direction of my abusers. My everyday life included constant exposure to pornography and almost daily sexualized engagement with Mr. Earl and many of his friends and associates.

Sugar and Spice

When the mail came, I held the gleaming Playboy magazine in my tiny hands excitedly, tracing the curvy body parts of whichever bombshell was gracing that month's cover, scanning the image for the hidden bunny that the graphic artist had skillfully concealed in the curls of the model's hair or the pattern on her thong bikini bottoms. My reward for finding the secret hidden bunny image was that I was allowed to open the three-page centerfold to admire the beautiful woman posed seductively in the middle of the magazine.

Children often have books or magazines they read or draw in, and I was no different, but my parents gave me pornography instead of coloring books. These magazines became my favorite things to look at, and I read every word of each one that came to our home. I was encouraged to study the ways the women were posed, and I had access to a closet full of clothes and high-heeled shoes I used to mimic them when my stepdad and his friends would set up photo and video shoots in his bedroom or our living room. They showed me pictures or videos detailing specific actions I should perform or poses I should hold and then happily responded when I did as I was instructed. Sometimes they rewarded me with presents like candy, clothes, or toys, but I only needed their positive affirmations to keep up the acts. They often had me mix whiskey cocktails and make myself sweet, fruity drinks to remove any of my hesitation or inhibitions.

One year, when I was ten or eleven years old, we received a special red-covered book or magazine in the mail. It was called "Sugar and Spice" and featured a little girl like me, posed nude in a steamy bathroom, with full make-up and styled hair. Her photos were mingled with other young women who looked like the ladies in the magazines that came to our house each month, but she was prepubescent. Her undeveloped body was a stark contrast to the voluptuous curves of some of the other girls in the book, but the common thread was that they looked very immature. They all had props and poses that increased the innocence factor.

The little girl who was photographed for the pornographic features had long, brown hair and bushy eyebrows, and she was made famous as an actress. Her mother acted as her agent, booking her as a star in movies and as an object of sexuality in the red book. I remember more than one occasion when one of my mother's or stepdad's friends had a chance to be alone with me, and they said something like, "You really do look just like her!" because I also had long, dark hair and bushy, brown eyebrows, as well as an undeveloped, childlike body.

These men had consumed the pornographic images of a child who had been sexualized, which sparked a desire in them that they were finally able to fulfill when they found me, a child sex slave who had been meticulously groomed by pedophiles to perform in any way they could conceive. I was a real-life version of the little girl whose photos they had lusted over, and because I was already trained, they could act out their sick fantasies in real life.

The little girl's photos in the red book have been circulating for decades. The deviant people who collect images of children being sexualized and abused have secret networks where they exchange this material. I often wonder if the images and photos made of me as a child are still being passed around by these perverted criminals.

LIGHTBULB MOMENT

 **Every time images or videos of my childhood sexual abuse are viewed, traded, or sold, I am violated again.**

Long Walks on the Beach

Trips to the beach were very different for me than they probably were for most of the families that load up their cars with pails, shovels, tents, and towels.

Around the time I turned ten, my mother started making thong bikinis to sell to the girls she worked with at the strip club. We worked together to build the bathing suits and then tried them on, spinning around with hands on our hips like models, blowing kisses. My mother taught me how to pose and showed me how to playfully flip my hair over my shoulder. This was like an arts and crafts project for us, and I craved her attention. I see so clearly now that this was part of my sexualization at a young age. My mother and Mr. Earl encouraged me to associate "being sexy" with wearing these string thong bikinis, even though I was only a young, prepubescent child.

Sometimes we loaded the bikinis into our van and set up a spot to sell the colorful suits on the beach. My mother had me wear one of the string bikinis with ruffles on the backside to disguise that it was a thong. She instructed me to walk up and down the beach, and if anyone asked me where I got the bathing suit, she wanted me to bring them back to the van.

One day, I was walking on the beach in my tuxedo thong bikini. It had a little bowtie on the back with little white flaps like the tails of a tuxedo, which ruffled around my rear end. As I walked along the beach, a man approached me and asked me where I got the bathing suit. That was my cue to take him to the van where my mother was waiting. She had bikinis hanging on the open back doors of the van, but when I brought him to her, she told me to wait on the other side of the van. She started talking to him, asking if he wanted the bathing suit for his girlfriend.

I didn't hear everything that was said, but soon, the man came around the side of the van to where I was, and he got into the van with me. My mother had closed the back doors, and there was a shelf like a bed built into the back of the van with carpet covering the walls. He thought this was the perfect place to abuse me.

Another time at the beach, there were lots of people because it was Spring Break. The atmosphere was more party-driven than family-friendly, and a local radio station was set up with a big stage and sound system. Bands were playing all day long, and a huge crowd was gathered. In the afternoon, the stage was used for a bikini contest, and the popular radio DJs worked to get the crowd pumped up.

My mother entered me in the bikini contest. I think I was ten years old, but all of the other women in the contest were grown-ups, like the pretty ladies in the magazines and videos at our house. I think some of the ladies in the contest worked at the strip club with my mother, and they danced around or did the splits when it was their turn to walk the catwalk. I was intimidated by all of these beautiful women who seemed so confident, strutting around almost naked in front of hundreds of strangers who were screaming obscenities. But I had experience from wearing bikinis at the country clubs and helping my mother sell the suits we made together, so I overcame my fear, wanting my mother and Mr. Earl to be proud of me.

When it was my turn to parade myself on the stage, I tried my best to shake my butt and run my hands up and down my body like the other contestants did. As I walked along the stage, the crowd was cheering, and I felt the energy of the horde of drunken, sunburnt partiers. The announcer said something like, "Be careful guys, twelve will get ya twenty!" and everyone burst out in peals of laughter. I didn't get that joke, and my mother had lied to the announcer because I wasn't twelve yet.

My mother was especially proud of the way I performed on the stage. She and Mr. Earl encouraged me to be open and expressive with my sexuality. I was like a magnet that brought them people who wanted a young girl like me, a child who was trained to be compliant and obedient. I have no idea what monetary value my actions were worth, but we lived in a beautiful, brand-new home in an upscale neighborhood with all of our needs being met.

The Same Street as the Junior High School

One reason Mr. Earl chose the house right down the street from the school was so I could bring little girls home with me when the school day was over. I learned that bringing the girls to my house at the end of the school day earned me rewards. It was easy for Mr. Earl to train my friends to comply because I was a real-life example who showed them what to expect when hanging out or spending the night at our house.

Many of the children I met when I was taken to yacht clubs or parties were also being sexually abused. This normalized the sexual contact with adults, but there was always a code of secrecy. There were things said to me and the other children that built our intimate trust of and fierce obedience to the abusers. This abuse was common to me, with many adults in many different places involved. It seemed like this was the way life must be for everyone.

One of the little girls I brought home to spend the night rejected the training Mr. Earl attempted to put her through, and she alerted a teacher about what she had experienced that evening at my house. That teacher called the cops, and when law enforcement responded, they secretly took me out of school to a police station downtown.

I wish I had been articulate enough to explain the situation to the detectives. If I had the language, I could have described how this "wealthy businessman" met my newly widowed mother when I was entering kindergarten, and how he saw his opportunity to procure me as his live-in child sex slave. I could have told them it didn't take him long to identify her needs and create the illusion of provision, safety, and security she was desperately searching for. I could have alerted them to why it's important to keep in mind that traffickers might target single mothers for easy access to their children.

This trafficker had used my mother's instability and insecurity as a way to become involved in my life, and she quickly became complicit in making me into a sexual object for him and his associates. Now, six years later, as a twelve-year-old seventh grader, I was with these two detectives who had a chance to help me.

Being all alone at the police station was a confusing and scary situation for me, and the little room they put me in was cold and stark. I was extremely careful about how I answered the questions the two male detectives asked, and I wanted to sound intelligent. I tried to remember what Mr. Earl had instructed me to say if I was ever interviewed by the police, but I forgot how I was supposed to answer. The officers told me not to tell anyone I had spoken to them—not my friend, not my mother, and especially not Mr. Earl.

By the end of that week, Mr. Earl was arrested.

His arrest triggered my mother to start culling resources and calling in favors from the network of powerful and wealthy people with whom they had created relationships. She sold some of our furniture and brought a special doctor to our house to interview me, but I think he actually hypnotized me. The dishonest doctor gave my mother a report that said I had not been abused but was hallucinating because I had a mental illness, just like my father.

My mother spoke harshly to me and accused me of ruining everything she had worked so hard for. She said we were going to be homeless because I couldn't keep my mouth shut. It was a desperate time, and she was drinking heavily and using drugs frequently. My life became unbearable, and hearing her constant threats and condemnation made me want to be anywhere but with her.

She worked to gather the finances to have Mr. Earl released from jail. He was placed on probation after entering a guilty plea. [1]

Mr. Earl had been locked up, but he didn't stay in jail long.

The justice system failed to protect me.

When he came home, I ran away.

---

[1] I have the entire file from Mr. Earl's court case, including my affidavit. This is a powerful tool to aid in training law enforcement to identify and respond to familial trafficking, child sexual abuse material, child sexual assault and molestation, and pedophilia.

Chapter 5

SURVIVAL ON THE STREETS
The Exploitation of a Preteen Runaway

12-13 years old

When everyone in a young girl's world has perpetrated abuse, it's impossible to find hope, trust, or stability.

Running away isn't just about trying to find somewhere safe to land; the force that drives someone forward is often the desire to escape the pain. I was only twelve years old, but I was so desperate to break free from the abuse that I ran away.

I ran.

I ran away from all of the men.

I ran away from the pornography that they used to train me.

I ran away from the drugs and alcohol I was given to make me compliant.

I ran away from all the people in my life who were supposed to protect me, defend me, and look after me, but who instead abused me and allowed me to be abused.

And I quickly learned a difficult reality.

The streets are a dangerous place for broken little girls.

Daddy's Girl Learned Fast

When I was twelve years old, after the arrest of Mr. Earl, my mother began selling our belongings. We couldn't afford to stay in the expensive neighborhood, and Mr. Earl's probation officer said he was not allowed to live with me anymore. Before long, she moved us out of the comfortable, newly built suburban home near the highly rated school. Instead, she found a dilapidated shack to rent on the rough side of town, just a few houses down from the busy, noisy interstate that bisected the city. This neighborhood felt dangerous and dirty, and the house we rented was infested with rodents and roaches.

My mother was drinking heavily, and at night, the pile of empty beer cans in the corner of the kitchen was like a playground for mice who would crawl through the crumpled aluminum clutter and create a cacophony of crunches and clattering. The scary sounds coming from the kitchen sometimes were drowned out by gunshots ringing in the alleys, and sleeping at that house was never easy.

One day, shortly after we moved in, my mother had a surprise waiting for me when I came home from school. She had arranged for Mr. Earl to be there, and he was sitting on the couch with a smirk on his face. My mother demanded I apologize to him for lying about him and trying to ruin his life and professional reputation.

Shocked and angry, I went into my bedroom, slammed the door, and hastily put some clothes and random items into my bag. Then, I went back through the living room where the two of them sat, ran past them, and straight out the front door. All I had in my backpack was a few personal things and no resources or money, but I ran away with no intention of ever returning. The situation I was facing at home was so impossible to navigate that it seemed better to take my chances on the streets. In my twelve-year-old mind, the only solution I could think of was running away.

Initially, I ran about a mile from the house to an abandoned Little League park. I slowed to a walk as I trekked diagonally across the field to a small building with a long bench running along the back wall, where I finally sat down to catch my breath. It felt like a safe place—like a shelter where I could hide. I leaned against the dugout wall, trying to think of a plan to get out of the mess I was in.

Years earlier, we had moved to this city, far away from Clayton and the rest of our family, and I felt isolated from them. I could not contact my grandmother or any of my other family members. Now, we had moved to the other side of town, away from the teachers I had built trust with at my school. I didn't have any way to reach out to them, either.

I felt worthless, and my life felt hopeless because I had nowhere to go.

Under the Bridge

After considering my options, I realized that I didn't have anyone to help me. I thought about giving up and returning home, so I left the dugout and started walking back toward the house. In my heart, I hoped to see my mother searching for me, calling out my name, and looking in ditches to see if I was hurt. But she wasn't looking for me. No one was looking for me.

As I made my way to a highway underpass just a couple of blocks away from the house my mother had rented, I came upon a strange scene. Homeless people and drug addicts begged for money along the sidewalks around the area. When cars stopped at the intersection, these hustlers would approach the driver's windows with their hands out, demanding that the person behind the wheel hand over cash.

I saw they also waited for customers to pull into the parking lot of the small convenience store near the highway overpass bridge. As people tried to enter or exit the store, the beggars harassed them until they forked over some change. The area felt charged with danger, and as a twelve-year-old little girl, I should have been more frightened than I was.

Swallowing my fear, I climbed up to the top of the concrete ramp to a little shelf-like area beneath the overpass where I hid from the scary people and tried to find safety. It was a rude awakening when I discovered there were rats, bats, and bugs making their home under the bridge as well. I had no other option but to make a camp there, and I used my backpack as a makeshift pillow.

That first night was scary, and the constant noise of cars speeding over top of me shook my body but also became like a lullaby to help me block out the creepy critters as I drifted off to a night of shallow sleep.

Feed Me and Gimme Shelter

The first evening that I slept on the streets, I found a half-eaten hot dog and some cold fries in a paper bag someone had tossed in the trash can. That was my dinner for the night. I felt gross digging the food out of the trash, but I also felt lucky that I had found something to eat that would silence my growling stomach. Sleeping under the scary bridge and digging my dinner from the garbage were better options than staying home and facing my mother's verbal assaults and the daily sexual abuse from Mr. Earl and his friends.

When I came down from the little cement shelf where I slept, it never took long for me to capture the attention of men driving through the underpass or along the service road. Men would pull over to talk to me with their hazard lights flashing. Sometimes they turned into the convenience store to flag me over to their cars. Most twelve-year-olds who had been taught "stranger danger" would have looked at these as dangerous situations, but as a little girl with no concept of risk, I innocently walked right up to their cars. I got into the passenger seat without ever suspecting anything except that these men were going to help me.

The men usually started by asking me if I needed help, if I was hungry, or if I needed a place to sleep or shower. They seemed nice, like they cared about me and wanted to help me. Sometimes they asked me if I wanted to get high, and to that, my answer was always, "Yes!" I had already learned how alcohol and drugs could numb my body and my mind, and as I became desperate to break free from the abuse, I just wanted to stay numb.

I was already groomed and had been programmed to expect adult men to expect sexual attention from me, and I knew I would receive rewards and praise for compliance. Without suspicion, I went with these men to wherever they took me, happy to be with someone who promised to meet my needs.

LIGHTBULB MOMENT

Runaways are vulnerable to being trafficked by opportunistic predators who coerce the child into trading sexual contact for items they need to survive, like food, shelter, or protection.

The men almost always asked me how old I was, and sometimes I lied and told them I was fourteen. I thought that if they knew the truth, they might try to call my mother or, worse, the police. I knew I was breaking the law by running away and skipping school, and I was concerned the police would make me go back to live with my mother and Mr. Earl. I was afraid the men might not help me if they knew I was only twelve years old.

Whether I told them I was twelve or fourteen was irrelevant because they would always get what they wanted from me. I usually got what I wanted, too, and they never called the police or made me go back to the place I was escaping from.

Paying the Price of a Yankee Dime

The corner convenience store by the bridge was like a godsend for me. I came down from my little cement shelf with my stomach growling and feeling so thirsty, and I decided to go into the little store and get something to fill my empty belly. Gathering my backpack, I made the short trek down to the rickety little shop.

When I went in the door, I felt the old man who worked the counter watching me like a hawk. I hoped he would be distracted by other customers paying for their items, so when one of them had his attention, I saw my chance and slipped a bag of chips into my backpack. I had never stolen anything before and was terrified of being caught, so I quickly turned around to get out of the store as fast as possible.

Trying to cut down the aisle closest to the door, I was abruptly stopped by the shopkeeper. He had a twisted smile on his face as he stood between me and the doorway, blocking my escape.

"Did you want to pay for that bag of chips, little girl?" he asked, his gnarled smile revealing missing teeth and black gums.

My head dropped. "I don't have any money," I stammered.

"Well, I'll tell ya what, young lady, if you want, I'll let you pay with a Yankee Dime, what do you say about that? And you can get anything else you want, too. How does that sound?" the man smiled.

I wasn't sure what he meant by a Yankee Dime, but I understood I wouldn't have to pay, which was a huge relief. So, I grabbed a sandwich and a candy bar, asking, "Can I have these for one of those Yankee Dimes, too?" A glimmer came across my young eyes.

"Sure, honey, help yourself to anything you want. Get a soda pop, too. Or would a girl like you rather have a can of beer?" he asked with a chuckle.

The thought of drinking a sour beer didn't appeal much to me, but I knew the alcohol would give my anxious body that calm, tingly feeling. I took the man up on his offer and grabbed one from the cooler. Once I gathered all my supplies into my backpack, he led me up to the counter.

He raised the divider to allow me to come back behind the register and waved me through a door into his tiny office. Giving me a boost, he set me up on the desk and made sure I had everything I had selected out in the storefront. I was so happy to have food and drink and be in a nice, safe place to eat. The man seemed pretty happy about the situation as well, but before I could open my bag of chips, he grabbed my hand and said, "Wait a minute, honey, you haven't paid for those yet."

"Oh yeah," I replied. "You wanted me to pay with play money. Here's your dime, mister," I joked as I pretended to drop an invisible coin into his hand.

"Oh no, no, my little friend. That's not a Yankee Dime; this is," he said slyly, leaning toward me and giving me a gruesome kiss as his hand went up the front of my shirt.

I was paralyzed and sat on the desk, frozen in time, the crumpled bag of chips still in my hand. Stone cold and still as a statue, I felt the old man's sticky tongue trying to poke itself between my lips as he panted against my face. He pressed his body against my tiny frame while his gruff hands groped for whatever they could find to grab. I felt my heart pounding in my throat, but I was so helpless I couldn't cry out or push the man away.

The chimes of the door opening and signaling a customer coming into the store were the only things that stopped the man's advances. He left me sitting up on the desk to go out and ring up the order, and as soon as I saw my chance, I slung my bag over my shoulder and bolted past the counter and right out the door.

I ran up under the bridge with my treasures, knowing I had unlocked a secret to survival. I didn't have to go for rides in cars with strange men if I could just walk across the service road and get food or candy or cigarettes from the little store.

Paying the man his Yankee Dimes became easier the more I went to get supplies. Over time, I learned some things were more expensive than others. He pushed me to allow him more access to my body for the pricier items. *My body was a commodity*, only good for getting my basic needs met. But at the end of the experience, it seemed fair to me. I got what I wanted, and so did he. Decades later, I wonder if he has nightmares of the exchanges like I still do.

Intersection with Law Enforcement and Medical Systems

During that time on the street, I was violently attacked and hit in the head with a crowbar—my skull cracked open. I was dumped at the front entrance of a hospital emergency room, covered in blood. I woke up the next morning with stitches in my head and my angry mother sitting next to me in a teen shelter. She took me home with her that day, but as soon as I was able to leave again, I ran away.

None of the doctors, nurses, or staff of the hospital or youth center asked me why I was running away, where I was getting money for food, where was I sleeping, how I was getting the drugs and alcohol I had in my system, or what was I doing in that alley behind a convenience store at 2 a.m.

All this time, men were having sexual contact with me, and none of them ever tried to help me by getting me off the streets. I did what I thought I had to do to survive. These men were criminals who saw their opportunity to exploit a child and get away with it.

Being at home with my mother meant being with Mr. Earl—and dealing with their anger toward me because of the mess I had caused by going to the police and giving my statement—so I continued to run away every chance I got. However, being on the streets instead of being in school during the day made me an easy target for law enforcement.

I was arrested or detained several times when I was twelve and thirteen. Whether I was taken back to my mother or the juvenile detention center (JDC), I never felt seen or heard. I became increasingly angry and distrustful of authority figures, especially the police. When I had court dates, I was usually disrespectful and displayed my anger to the judge, which often resulted in little mercy from the bench. One court date, a judge declared that I was an unruly child; another time, I was labeled as delinquent, and after that, I was either placed in a behavioral hospital or locked up in JDC, which was like being in jail.

Because I usually had alcohol and drugs in my system when I was arrested, the judge once ordered me to attend ninety Alcoholics Anonymous (AA) meetings in ninety days. I had a form the judge wanted signed by the leader each time I went to a meeting, and I sometimes went to three meetings in a day because I wanted to get the whole process over with. As far as I understood, AA meetings were just a bunch of people hanging out for an hour, smoking cigarettes, and drinking coffee with too much sugar. Sometimes a small group of us went to a diner for pie after the meetings, but everyone there was at least two or three times my age. I didn't fit into the crowd because I was only a twelve-year-old little girl.

At one of the meetings, I was approached by a man in his thirties who offered to be my "sponsor." I didn't know any better than to accept his offer. Instead of mentoring me in how to follow the principles within the AA organization, he took me to his run-down trailer and gave me peppermint schnapps and LSD so he could keep me under his control for several days.

One day, when the man from AA left to buy food and alcohol, I went into his bathroom and used a disposable razor to shave off the sides of my long, dark hair into a mohawk. Once he returned, he was angry to see how I had changed my appearance. He told me he had heard from someone that the cops were looking for me, so he took me downtown and dropped me off on a street corner.

I was still high from all the drugs my "AA sponsor" had given me over those several days, and I went into a barbershop to ask the barber to help me finish shaving my head. Seeing the lice crawling on my bare scalp, the old man was visibly disturbed. He had mercy on me and used a set of clippers to clean up the mess I had made before he sent me on my way with a black plastic comb in my back pocket.

Soon after, I was picked up by a man who violently raped me at knifepoint. When it was almost time for the sun to come up, he dumped me out of his car in an upscale neighborhood near the bayfront. The ritzy homes had spacious lawns and lush landscaping, and I attempted to hide my nude body behind the bushes along a mansion's front porch. As I crept along from house to house, I made my way to the corner of the street where I noticed a dry cleaner in a little shopping center.

Realizing the dry cleaner would have clothes I could put on to cover my nakedness, I attempted to sneak through the back door, but the staff was already working in the rear of the shop. When they saw me, they were clearly concerned and brought me a big blanket to wrap myself in as they called the police. Once the police came, I was taken to the pediatric children's hospital where a rape kit was completed by a Sexual Assault Nurse Examiner (SANE). After the SANE exam, my mother was called to pick me up from the hospital. I ran away again as soon as I could.

There were other times when the judge referred me to a Mental Health/Mental Rehabilitation (MHMR) facility or a drug rehabilitation clinic. While living for a month in the drug rehab clinic, I met other young people who were surviving on the streets. I learned a lot from them about places to sleep and ways to get money or food.

The teenagers I met at the JDC were much more criminally minded than the ones from the rehab clinic. The JDC crowd was made up of gang bangers who had stolen cars or kids who had been caught with guns or selling drugs. Fights often broke out. Even though I had a mohawk and would wear smudged eyeliner, black nail polish, and dark lipstick, I was not tough. I was afraid of them.

At the MHMR facility, the aides did their best, attempting to get me to engage in art therapy or music classes, but I was disrespectful, and my anger raged. Once, when I was being punished for bad behavior, the staff locked me in a room. I kicked and punched holes in the drywall, then ripped down big pieces of the walls and pulled out the electrical outlets and light switches, destroying the property.

Claiming I was schizophrenic like my father, my mother worked hard to have me admitted to the county mental ward, and after two weeks there, I was placed in the state mental hospital. This was a place for the criminally insane, and I was surrounded by people who had hurt and even killed people but had no remorse. I have memories of a doctor coming to the hospital, and the nurses helped him strap me to the bed before performing an abortion on me. I didn't even know I was pregnant, and I believe my mother was involved in setting this up. I bled heavily for many days after the procedure; meanwhile, the staff kept me doped up on the psychiatric medication Thorazine as well as other drugs.[1]

Every time I was arrested, Mr. Earl's lies were reinforced in my mind. He had warned me that if I ever told anyone what was happening, I would get locked up and never see my family again. It was an easy decision to run away because I did not want to be around him or my mother, and since she wanted to be with him, he was usually at the house. When the police picked me up, they took me to the JDC, the mental health care facility, or a drug rehab clinic, and I would be behind bars, confirming the threats my stepdad had made.

As a broken twelve-year-old child, I lashed out at police and others who were in positions of power. I violently resisted them, cussing, spitting, kicking, and punching to avoid being taken into custody. I had no language to express to them what a dire situation I was in, and I had no way of explaining to them why I would rather sleep under a bridge than at my mother's home. In a very childish way, I acted out with disobedience as a way of crying for help, but my behavior was never correctly interpreted. Instead, I became trapped in the revolving system. My angry outbursts usually led to more charges and an extended time of being locked up.

The disrespect I showed was a sign that something was very wrong in my world, but no one seemed able to break through my defenses and connect with me on a heart level. My anger was like a shield, but it would turn into a weapon if I thought I was going to be sent back to my mother and Mr. Earl or be placed in a facility again.

Unfortunately, the places the police took me were not properly equipped or trained to help me deal with the damage from the years of sexual abuse and trafficking that I had endured. It seemed as if no one in those institutions was able to help me. They just used drugs or restraints to keep me under control until they could release me or transfer me to the next location. When it was time to leave one of those facilities, I would be released to my mother's care and would run away again at my first opportunity.

When There Is No Place to Go

When I was sleeping on the streets, I just wanted enough drugs to make my pain go away. I was only twelve years old, but I searched for alcohol and was desperate for a place to sleep besides under a bridge or in a baseball dugout. I wanted food other than what I was digging out of trash cans. The men who offered to help me knew I was in a devastating situation.

Any time somebody exchanged a sexual act for anything of value with me as a child, it was technically trafficking. It might be called "survival sex" in the case of a runaway who is just trying to survive. But the exchange of *anything* of value with a minor for a sex act is considered trafficking under federal law.[2]

I learned the hard way that you can't always trust people, even when you want to. I was exploited and abused by scores of men, many of whom were in positions of authority or trust in their communities. Many of them were businessmen who had the respect of their peers—men who were in leadership positions.

These were people who should have known better.

People who should have protected me.

It's hard to trust anyone when the people you're supposed to trust are adding to your exploitation. With the information I have now, it's easy to see them as monsters, but at the time, I viewed them very differently. Instead of seeing the red flags, I saw them as heroes solving my problems, like an answer to my prayers.

Those incidents led to deep wells of shame that I felt like I was drowning in. With no hope and nowhere to go, I found myself subjected to men who continued to victimize me and take advantage of my vulnerabilities, keeping me trapped in the cycle of trauma and humiliation.

As a child runaway at just twelve years old, I encountered what I now realize was an endless stream of enterprising traffickers and opportunistic predators who were constantly using my desperation and vulnerability to cater to their deviant physical desires. I was a convenient, pre-trained tool to help fulfill their lustful fantasies of sex with a little girl who didn't have any defense or protection. Sadly, this is still happening every day in the communities we live in.

Children are being sold for sex on the streets of the cities and towns we live in. We need to bring an end to this. We must work to make our children and other vulnerable people safe in our cities and towns.

Everything I had ever seen, everything I had ever experienced up to that point, had been exploitation. I was the perfect victim for predators because I had been meticulously groomed and conditioned for years. I was like a gold mine for traffickers because they knew how to use my brokenness for their financial benefit.

Because I received no healing from the abuse, my heart hardened toward authority figures. I became bent on self-destructive behavior. As you'll read in the upcoming chapters, throughout my teens and early twenties, I was trapped in a cycle of drug abuse, depression, failed relationships, and continued victimization by pimps, sugar daddies, drug dealers, and men I thought were boyfriends. But I see now they were traffickers.

My story could have been quite different.

Maybe, if I had encountered people who cared about my healing when I was a young victim of sex trafficking, I could have received the much-needed care, counseling, and healing from the trauma I endured. The care and support of a committed group of therapists and counselors might have been exactly what I needed to break the cycle and find freedom from the shame and stigma of the abuse and exploitation I had undergone.

A safe family setting built on trust and mutual respect, where healthy choices are encouraged and honor is established, may have given me a way out of this destructive cycle. But, instead of finding a family, the next man who took advantage of me was another "father figure" who fueled my young life with sex, drugs, and rock 'n' roll.

---

[1] I have the entire medical record of my stay at this hospital, including handwritten notes from staff members each day. This is a powerful tool for training medical professionals who may encounter a trafficking victim.

[2] U.S. Department of Justice: Criminal Division. "Citizen's Guide to U.S. Federal Law on Child Sex Trafficking." August 11, 2023. https://www.justice.gov/criminal/criminal-ceos/citizens-guide-us-federal-law-child-sex-trafficking.

Chapter 6

BIKERS AND BONFIRES

The Cocaine Can't Pay for Itself

14-16 years old

After more than a year of running away, being locked up in juvenile detention centers, drug rehab clinics, and mental health facilities, and spending a short stint in foster care, I was placed back into my mother's custody. She had recently given birth to a new baby and now was responsible for three daughters.[1] The courts had ordered Mr. Earl to stay away from me, and my mother was not able to support us on her own, so we left the Gulf Coast and Mr. Earl behind. We drove for days and returned to Clayton, moving back into my grandparents' home. My grandpa was still working at the factory, but now he had even more mouths to feed.

The poverty surrounding us in Clayton was depressing. We had experienced a very different financial situation for the six years we were with Mr. Earl, and my mother was motivated to find another man to provide the affluent lifestyle she had become accustomed to. She kept in touch with Mr. Earl, but shortly after we moved back to our hometown, she found a new man, and the cycle of sexual exploitation and abuse continued in my life.

My mother's new husband, Billy, was networked with hard-core bikers and international drug dealers. He and my mother found a house for rent in Clayton, and we moved out of my grandparents' house. Once they were married, our lifestyle revolved around biker bars, clubhouses, and parties. Billy didn't own a motorcycle, but he always had a supply of hard liquor, beer, and marijuana; cocaine was his favorite drug of choice. Even though I was only fourteen when he and my mother got together, Billy often included me in partying with booze, weed, and hard drugs like cocaine.

Before long, Billy became physically abusive to my mother, and our house was transformed into a war zone. Two of his daughters had come to live with us, which meant we had five young girls under one roof, with me as the oldest at fourteen and the others ranging in age from just a couple of years younger than me to my new baby sister, who was born when I was thirteen.

This life didn't revolve around fancy boats and country clubs. It was gritty and harsh and, at times, dangerous and scary. I would especially worry about my baby sister, who was always in the middle of chaos. There was no routine or family rhythm except for daily drunkenness and debauchery from the adults in charge.

Billy spent a lot of time with me, and we made jokes about how my mother was a lightweight. Sometimes when we were just hanging out at home, we would all smoke a joint, and she would get so high that she passed out. Billy and I stayed awake, playing '70s rock music, smoking pot, and drinking into the night. If some of my young teenage girlfriends wanted to come hang out with us, he was always happy to get them high, too. If they were lucky, especially if they were cute, he sent them home with some booze or weed.

Get Your Motors Runnin'

There were times when Billy and my mother took me to a biker party or weekend camping trip where scores of rough-and-tough men and women would be partying, drinking, using drugs, and shooting guns. At first, I was intimidated by this scene, but it quickly became normal to me, and I started seeing where I fit into these scenarios.

Heading to a weekend of camping meant stopping at the liquor store to fill up a cooler with beer and ice and buying some bottles of whiskey, vodka, and tequila. I liked sweet, creamy alcoholic drinks like Bailey's Irish Cream or Tequila Rose (which was Pepto-Bismol-pink and tasted like candy), so Billy and my mother always got those for me to drink. We also stocked up on cigarettes and rolling papers for smoking pot.

Trying to be edgy, I wore cut-off denim shorts and tight, skimpy tops. I put makeup on my face and accentuated my eyes with mascara; my lips and cheeks were red from rouge and lipstick. My long, brown hair fell down my back almost to my waist, and while I was just a fourteen-year-old girl, I looked and acted much older. My rough experiences as a runaway had left me street-smart and shrewd, but inside, I was just a lost little girl surrounded by adults who failed to protect and provide safety for me. My tough exterior was just a facade.

When we showed up at whichever campground we were heading to, the party was already rolling with music blasting and people all around the property drinking and dancing. After we set up a tent or fixed the backseat of our car as a makeshift bed, we started mingling with the crowd and grabbed some food or shared some drinks with the partygoers.

There were usually people passing around marijuana joints, which sometimes were laced with angel dust or PCP, potent psychedelic drugs that cause hallucinations. The adults didn't seem concerned about the illegal activities because it was a private event on private property. The free-for-all vibe of these types of events made it feel like a safe place for other underage girls and me to openly drink and get high. My mother and

Billy encouraged me to let my guard down and cut loose. After all, it was a party, and everyone was there to get drunk and high and have a good time.

It was common for Billy and the other men at these parties to have cocaine, and even though everyone knew what was going on, they would be secretive and snort the powder only inside a tent or someone's car. It seemed shifty and shady to sneak off to a corner somewhere, but I was always happy to creep around if it meant I could get high. The secrets Billy and I shared about cocaine made us more connected and created a deeper bond. To him, I was an attention magnet. He knew that wherever he brought me, he would benefit.

The atmosphere at these events was high and happy, and there was a constant flow of booze, pot, and drugs. I especially liked how the cocaine numbed me and made me want to dance all night long. If I danced provocatively, I would hear cheers from the men watching me. I thought I was acting like the ladies in the videos I had been shown since kindergarten, but a child can't be seductive or sexy.

It didn't seem to matter that I was only fourteen or fifteen years old; I was the center of the men's attention. These predators encouraged me to channel the sex appeal I had been trained to emulate from being shown porn since I was six years old.

LIGHTBULB MOMENT

Children who display sexually-charged cues are not being flirtatious or promiscuous; they are victims of child abuse who have been broken by predators. These signals are interpreted by other abusers as signs that the child will make a submissive, compliant victim.

Once the sun went down and the bonfire was lit, the party rolled on, and more drugs and drinking meant more inhibitions were removed. I ended up in the car or tent with Billy and one of his friends who had cocaine. After we snorted the powder, my stepdad went back to the party, and I was left alone with the man in the backseat of his car or the sleeping bag in his tent. It took decades for me to realize that I was the payment for the drugs I had done with my parents.

Paint it Black

These nights blurred into a chaotic haze of drunkenness and indulgence. I found myself in situations that I didn't want to be a part of, but I had no way out. I often woke up the following morning filled with shame.

One morning after a wild night, I came to as the sun was rising, naked and wrapped in a sheet, face down in the grass near a pond. I had grass and bugs tangled in my hair, and my makeup was smeared across my face with crusty, dried vomit. Another morning, I woke up in the back of a van with a big, hairy man snoring next to me. Even though I couldn't remember all the things that had happened in the long nights before those agonizing mornings, I felt like I had barely survived to see the next day.

One time, I went to find my mother to get a cigarette, and she laughed at me, commenting how it looked like I had a good time the night before, as she handed me some wet wipes to clean myself up. She made coffee and Bloody Marys to start the day, and someone using a giant skillet over the fire fried up eggs, bacon, and pancakes for the early risers. We slowly ate breakfast and nursed our headaches, feeling rough the morning after a night of revelry.

At one of these biker bashes, my mother taught me a hack to get rid of a hangover, and she swore that it worked every time. She dug a cold can of Coca-Cola out of the cooler—it had to be a can, not a bottle or fountain drink—and cracked it open, raised it to her lips, turned it upside down, and chugged it in just one or two gulps. Presto—hangover gone!

My mother may have never taught me how to cook or clean, but she showed me how to make a Bloody Mary, take a tequila shot with salt and lime, and cure a hangover with a can of Coke or a line of cocaine.

These stories might not sound like a normal family camping trip, but situations like this were normal for me. All I ever knew was sexualization and abuse, and I had been taught by the adults in my life that I should use my body to get attention, provision, protection, and all the drugs I would ever be able to do.

Baby, You Can Drive My Car

As I got closer to sixteen years old, I wanted to get my driver's license. Billy offered to teach me how to drive a stick shift in his car. He had a five-speed Mustang, but it was a junky car with a lot of mechanical issues and an ugly paint job. But, still, it was a Mustang.

One winter night, we had been partying with his friends in a town about a half-hour drive from Clayton. I was driving Billy's Mustang on the way back to our house, and he was telling me when to mash the gas or stomp the clutch as he shifted the gears. When we came around a 90° curve at a high rate of speed, the car went off the road, coming to a stop after spinning a few donuts in the snowy field. We laughed so hard, but reality set in when we had to walk through the field without winter coats. We hitchhiked the rest of the way home.

Billy and my mother were seldom home, and my sisters and I figured out how to survive on our own, find food, and take care of each other. Because there was rarely an adult supervising us, our house became the hotspot for our friends to hang out, especially the teenage boys. While I tried to be a responsible big sister, I often got drunk or high, which left all of us vulnerable.

The factory Billy worked at was forty-five minutes away, so he left by six in the morning to make his shift. Every morning, he would stop to pick up a six-pack of beer to drink on the way to the plant, saving a couple in his pail to guzzle on his lunch break. Driving with a beer can between his legs was a common practice, even on his way to work before the sun rose.

There were multiple times when Billy would drive home drunk. One night, my mother was passed out upstairs in her bed, and Billy had passed out in another area of the house. He was often naked when he passed out, and more than once, I found him on the staircase. My bedroom was in the basement, and I sometimes wondered if he was trying to get to my room in the middle of the night.

After a couple of years stuck in this dysfunctional life, I decided I didn't want to live like that anymore and found a way out of the situation—and into a much more dire circumstance.

---

[1] As I share the details of my story, I am careful to refer only to the abuse I personally experienced. It is not my place to discuss the details of my sisters' childhoods. It is important to note that sometimes pedophiles and child abusers will choose to target one child in the family to groom and assault, and the other children in the home will not be abused.

Chapter 7

PICKED UP AT THE PUBLIC POOL
Targeted, Tricked, and Trapped by a Trafficker

16-18 years old

When I was a teenager, my older "boyfriend" was a pimp who trafficked me for money and drugs. The addictions, abuse, and displacements I struggled with made me a walking goldmine for men like him with evil motives. Once he had me under his control, he used my fear, guilt, and shame to make it almost impossible to escape from his clutches. But the abusive, exploitative relationship did not start as the nightmare that it eventually became. Let's pick up where we left off, and you'll see what I mean.

On a sunny summer day, I was at Clayton's public swimming pool, lounging in my bikini. I had just turned sixteen, and I was daydreaming of breaking free from my crazy, dysfunctional life. I was ready to start on a path of my choosing. I wanted a hero to rescue me from my mother, and I didn't want to live in a house where I found my naked stepdad passed out on his way to my bedroom in the middle of the night.

Like Offering Candy to a Baby

As luck would have it, I received the answer to my uninformed prayers in quite an unexpected way. A boy I knew from high school came up to the other side of the chain-link fence that surrounded the rectangular concrete pool. He waved at me and called me over. The kid was a couple of years older than I was, and he was popular with the stoners because he usually had beer, booze, or weed.

He asked me if I wanted to get high, which was exactly what I was hoping for. Pointing at a small, gray car parked next to the playground about 100 yards away, he told me his friend thought I was cute and wanted to meet me. He said his friend had some beer and good drugs in his car, so if I wanted to party with them, I should grab my things and meet them in the park.

I slid into my denim cut-off shorts, tank top, and flip-flops, grabbed my towel, and was through the gate and walking to meet these two guys in no time flat. When I got to the car, I was surprised to see the driver wasn't a high-school-age boy—but a man in his 30s—and he was in no way attractive. He kind of looked like Mr. Earl and was pale and fat with reddish hair, freckles, and pimples on his face. His car didn't look as great as it had from a distance, and I saw that it was scratched up along the side, the windshield was cracked, and it had a donut tire on the back passenger side.

The driver, whom I will call Mr. Ed, flashed a crusty smile at me and asked if I wanted to party with them. He said they had some beer and weed, and if I wanted to "take a trip," he had some LSD. That was all it took for me to get into the passenger seat of the car to disappear from the watching eyes of everyone milling around the park and pool. By the time we were exiting through the south gate, I had a square of paper soaked with LSD melting on my tongue and a cold beer between my legs.

This was not an abduction. I willingly got into his car, and Mr. Ed drove away from the public park. There were scores of people watching as I rode off with the two men who were notorious for doing drugs and hanging out with underage girls. It was not a secret that I left with them that day, and word travels fast in a small town.

The boarded-up businesses along Main Street told the sad story of Clayton's poverty as we drove past and headed into the hills on the outskirts of town. Mr. Ed took a sharp turn to explore the back roads, and before long, we pulled onto a property at the top of a hill on the edge of town.

Ten Years Have Got Behind Me

There were several vehicles parked down a short driveway from the road and hidden from sight for anyone driving by. A group of teens and young adults was milling around behind the cluster of parked cars, and once Mr. Ed parked, we got out to join them. The party atmosphere was charged, and everyone seemed high and happy. One of the cars had its doors open, and music was blasting from the radio. People were drinking, smoking weed, and laughing.

I recognized some of the people from my high school, but most of them were older or had graduated, and I wasn't on a first-name basis with them. Everyone seemed to know the guys I was with, and as we started mingling with the crowd, the LSD we had taken a short while before started to take effect.

Everything seemed to become elastic and was stretching and twisting. I felt weak and afraid and drew as close to Mr. Ed as I could get. He laughed as he pulled me closer to his side, and he started whispering things in my ear. He told me I was his girl; he had chosen me. He said he would take care of me, and I didn't have anything to worry about as long as I stuck with him. He added that I needed to be a good girl and do what he told me to do, and that he would make sure I was following his instructions.

After spending the day partying and drinking as we cruised the backroads, he took every opportunity to speak to me craftily and planted powerful patterns in my thoughts. He was firm but kind, and his words were direct and clear, but in my intoxicated state, I was unable to discern his motivation.

As the day was drawing to a close, about eight hours after he had picked me up, Mr. Ed pulled up to the same place we had met earlier that day. As he parked next to the swing set on the playground, he told me it was time for me to go home for the night. He gave me a specific time and place to meet him the next day.

Before he pulled away, he said, "You're my girl now, and I don't want you hanging out with any other dudes. If you talk to any other dudes, I'll kick their ass, and then I'll kick yours, too, you understand?" I nodded in agreement, still feeling the powerful influence of the drugs on my body and mind.

This man promised to take care of me and protect me, and, most importantly, he promised that if I hung out with him every day, I would have all the drugs I would ever want.

LIGHTBULB MOMENT

 **Traffickers often use illicit drugs to groom their victims by creating dependence or fostering addiction.**

He's a Loser, Baby

The next day, I met him at the appointed place and time—an alley a few blocks from my house, hidden from view for anyone driving down Clayton's main drag. I felt sneaky and sly, and the way my heart pounded and the adrenaline flowed was like a drug in my system. Once I was in his car, Mr. Ed sped off, and we headed to the backroads on the opposite side of town. When we were out in the middle of nowhere, he pulled off the road and parked behind a row of bushes that acted like a barrier to hide the view of the car from the road.

He pulled out a baggie of weed and a tiny plastic bag of white powder. Using his fingernail as a makeshift spoon, he scooped a mound of powder out of the bag and snorted it, then loaded up more and lifted it to my nose. Once I had inhaled the cocaine through my nostril, Mr. Ed rolled a joint, dusting it with powder from the tiny bag as he prepared it. Smoking that joint made me feel different from any other drug I had ever done, and I experienced sensations of floating.

Over the next few weeks, Mr. Ed shared some of his history with me and took me to lots of places, introducing me to people as "his girl." It seemed like no one had a problem with this thirty-something-year-old man having a sixteen-year-old girlfriend. During that time, Mr. Ed disclosed to me that he had spent several years in prison after he had beaten an elderly couple, tied them up, and stolen their Social Security checks. He laughed as he talked about defecating on their coffee table.

Besides lacking moral character, Mr. Ed was also not attractive to me in any way. He not only looked similar to my abusive stepdad, but just like Mr. Earl, Mr. Ed also had bad breath and body odor. In spite of my lack of attraction to him, I was deeply connected to him on a psychological level. I thought of him all day long and constantly considered whether a choice I was making would please him or make him angry. And while it only happened a few times over our nearly two-year-long relationship, I did not want to anger him because the level of violence he unleashed on me was terrifying.

The rest of that summer, I spent every day with Mr. Ed. Before my mother left for work, I pretended to go to the swimming pool or park, but instead, I cut through the alley and met him behind a neighbor's garage. The excitement never wore off, and I was as addicted to the adrenaline rush of sneaking around as I was to the illicit substances we consumed.

Mr. Ed was always reliable; he never missed a day of hanging out with me, was always on time to pick me up, and always dropped me off in the alley before dark. Every day, we drank beer or liquor and smoked weed, and it was common for us to snort cocaine, take a hit of LSD, or swallow a prescription pill like Vicodin or Percocet. This might sound like an unbelievably wild life for a sixteen-year-old girl, but I had already experienced so much dysfunction and abuse that it seemed like a perfectly natural situation to me.

Free to Do What I Want

Because I turned sixteen and was finally able to get my driver's license and a car that summer, Mr. Ed encouraged me to work at a fast-food restaurant in Jamestown, the small city nearby. I had a huge fight with my mother, and soon after, I went to live with Mr. Ed at his apartment between Clayton and Jamestown.

I often went to check on my little sisters and make sure they had food. Since there wasn't much food in the kitchen of my mother's house and there were four young girls living there, I usually spent my meager paycheck to buy groceries for them.

We went to the tiny community grocery shop and stocked up with loaves of bread and lunchmeat, bags of potatoes, and packages of ground beef. I let my sisters pick their favorite plastic-wrapped snack cakes and candy bars, and I grabbed boxes of cereal and jugs of milk to fill up the refrigerator and pantry.

My anger boiled when we put the food away because it seemed like there was always beer in the fridge but not much for the kids to eat. There might be a Styrofoam box of restaurant leftovers from somewhere Billy and my mother had eaten when she got off work at the bar she tended, but they didn't usually have anything else except bottles of ketchup, mustard, or jars of pickles and peppers.

Going to school and working at the fast-food place didn't leave a lot of time for hanging out with my sisters, but I drank or got high with Mr. Ed at his apartment every night. Looking back in light of what I know now,

I can see that my working at the fast-food spot was a way Mr. Ed could keep tabs on me while he groomed other girls. Whether I was at school or work, he kept track of my schedule and always knew where I would be. That way, he knew when to expect me to show up at the apartment so he could get the other girls out before my arrival.

LIGHTBULB MOMENT

 **Traffickers often have more than one victim at any given time, and they might have several targets they are simultaneously assessing.**

I Got a Fast Car

Mr. Ed bought a slick Camaro, complete with ground effects and a sporty spoiler. He sent me to school driving his car and often put some weed or pills in the console, encouraging me to share the drugs with the other girls at my high school who liked to party. He told me to bring them back to the apartment so we could all get high together. There were a few other girls my age who, like me, had been abused as young girls, and they were happy to come with me to party.

Whenever I brought a girlfriend home, Mr. Ed called one of his friends over to hang out, too. That meant two or three men in their thirties or forties were in an apartment in the middle of the small town, getting high and drunk with a couple of high school girls who were only fifteen or sixteen. We usually ended up doing whatever the men wanted before the night was over.

Girls like us wanted to get numb on booze and dope, and Mr. Ed and his buddies knew it. We were desperate for protection and were seeking a relationship with a father figure. We seemed to constantly attract older men who would keep us high and turn violent or force us to earn money for more drugs. I honestly thought some of those men were my boyfriends, but now that I can look back and see the truth, I know they were traffickers.

When I was seventeen, Mr. Ed, in a fit of anger and rage, repeatedly bashed my head into the concrete sidewalk, and I ended up in the hospital emergency room to have staples put in my skull. None of the doctors, nurses, or medical staff asked me what had happened, how I was getting the drugs and alcohol I had in my system, or who the thirty-something-year-old man with me was.

I was only seventeen years old, and Mr. Ed was obviously not my parent. This man had done prison time for violent crimes, didn't have a real job, and always had drugs and teenage girls around him, but no one at the hospital tried to find out why he was there. Someone in scrubs could have been my hero and given me a pathway out of that dangerous life, but no one made the heart connection with me. They just put the staples in my head and discharged me to leave with him.

When we were in his Camaro on the ride back to his apartment, I started thinking about how much I wanted to find a way out of the toxic relationship. It wasn't long before I was able to get free from Mr. Ed, but the next man I was with almost killed me several times. I was lucky to survive the year I spent in hell at his hands.

Chapter 8

CAUGHT IN A TRAP
At the End of a Dead-End Road

18 years old

I hated the big, blue baseball cap, itchy polo shirt, and too-long uniform pants I had to wear every day at the fast-food joint. I always smelled like greasy fries and onion rings, and the dorky outfit was way too big for me, even in size small. As much as I despised the ensemble, my boss at the restaurant put me at the front counter to take orders from the customers.

There Goes My Hero

One afternoon, about a month before my high school graduation, a dark-haired, older man came in to order food. He immediately started flirting with me, and while he seemed nice, it was obvious he was much older than I. He didn't seem to care that I was still a minor (even though I was almost eighteen). I was instantly attracted to how he presented himself as strong and confident. I later learned he was almost thirty, and he had just gotten out of prison for the second time in his adult life. But the day I met him, he seemed like he didn't have a care in the world—except making me smile.

He told me his name was Chad, and he charmed me from day one. He gushed about how pretty he thought I was and said if I was his girl there would be no way he would let me work in a place where scumbags could flirt with me. He informed me I deserved to have a good life and a good man who would take care of me and buy me perfume and flowers.

Chad started coming in every time I worked, and I took breaks from my shift to sit with him and drink a soda so we could talk and get to know each other better. Sometimes he brought me some weed, a piece of candy, or a single flower. He told me to enjoy the gifts but instructed me to throw them away before I went home to my boyfriend's apartment because he didn't want to get me in trouble. We sat in the corner and shared some fries, and Chad insulted my boyfriend, saying Mr. Ed must be a loser.

Each time Chad came to visit, he charmed me and spent an hour or more watching me work. He told me he had never seen a prettier girl in his whole life, announcing he was falling in love with me. He even said he wanted to share everything he had with me.

This sounded *too good to be true*, and this man had gone out of his way to show me affection and shower me with love. Chad seemed so genuine and honest about his feelings for me. Plus, he was way stronger than Mr. Ed, who had beaten me up and busted my head open just a couple of months earlier. When I finally found the courage to tell Chad about the day my boyfriend assaulted me, he became visibly angry and threatened to kill him if I didn't leave right then and come home with him forever.

So, I quit my job in the middle of my shift and went with him that night, following him to his house in my beat-up car.

A Single-Wide Slice of Paradise

"This is it! My own personal paradise!" Chad proclaimed as he opened my driver's door so I could exit my vehicle. A cacophony of barks was rising from the pit bulls he kept in a row of cages next to the garage. I was the tiniest bit afraid, but I tried hard not to show it.

We went up to the trailer house, and Chad showed me around the small space. There wasn't much to see. He had a coal stove rigged up with a metal pipe twisted and poked through the side of the wall. Assuring me the place stayed plenty warm in the winter, even if it snowed, he told me he would teach me how to build a fire when the time came.

That night, we slept together in his bed, and he told me he was going to hold me forever. He spread his hands across my back, and they were so large they nearly covered my entire back side-to-side from my shoulders to my waist. He seemed so strong, like a giant, and I pictured him as a protector. Being so young and desperate for safety and security, I was unable to see the subtle signs of danger he displayed.

The next day, he had me skip school, and he followed me to Mr. Ed's apartment in the middle of the day. Chad sat in his car while I pulled up and ran inside to get my things. It was just our luck that Mr. Ed wasn't there, and while I didn't have much, I was happy to get what clothes, makeup, and trinkets I did have.

On the way back to Chad's trailer, he stopped at his parents' house, and his mom, Karen, stocked me up with shampoo, soap, and makeup. Karen sold these personal care products through a home delivery catalog, and she let me pick whatever scents and colors I liked, making me feel like a princess. She said she was happy to know there would be another woman living on the property and encouraged me to come see her for coffee in the mornings. However, once I let her know I was still in high school, she was not happy with her son at all. She told Chad he was going to end up back in prison, but he didn't seem fazed by her angry correction.

The trailer we lived in was small, dingy, and run-down, but I did my best to turn it from sad and shabby to sparkling clean. Karen gave me some of her catalog company's cleaning supplies and pretty little seasonal decorations to help brighten the place up.

In the beginning, much of my time living with Chad was peaceful, and for the first few weeks, life seemed pretty good, even if a little lonely. I went to my final weeks of high school during the day, and Chad went to work odd jobs or did buying, selling, and trading with supplies and materials he came across one way or the other. No matter how he spent his days, once I headed home from school, I knew he was on his way to greet me.

One night, Chad came home in an odd mood, and, for seemingly no reason, he attacked me and beat me senselessly. Looking back, I think he was probably on crystal meth, and he was out of control, furiously punching me and screaming. With his giant hands, he wailed on me with his fists and threw me around like a rag doll. His anger raged, and he beat me until I bled and my face and body ached, covered with bruises.

Trapped Like a Rat in a Cage

After that night, much of the time, Chad held me captive in his house like a slave. He locked the door from the outside with a padlock and left me there for two or three days at a time, and when he came back, he was angry and violent. Sometimes he was hallucinating from doing drugs for days, and he thought I was an enemy he had to fight or kill.

There were times when Chad loaded his .22 pistol and stuck the long, silver barrel down my throat with his finger on the trigger. He used the gun to smack me in the side of the head to knock me out. Perhaps the scariest thing he did was put both of his big hands around my tiny neck as he strangled me until I passed out. When I regained consciousness, he was standing over me, cursing, yelling, and continuing to beat me with his fists and other objects.

I can't count how many times he choked me until he knocked me out. When I came to, it usually felt like I was dropping back into my body, and waves of terror would wash over me as I reacclimated. I had giant bruises on my face and body for weeks, and they turned shades of black and blue, then green and brown, and finally yellow as they started to fade away.

It was no mystery that Chad was obsessed with his many guns. He stood in the doorway of his trailer and looked out on the acres of field between his doorstep and the edge of the woods. When a deer emerged from the row of trees, he shot it with his AK-47.

He didn't shoot at only deer in the yard; one time, he shot at me as I tried to run away. I zigzagged through the driveway to escape the hail of bullets flying at me. Once, I hid behind a broken-down van in the yard, and Chad shot the tires out as I crouched behind them. I felt like I lived in a war zone and never knew if I would survive to see the next day.

Changing My Smile Forever

One night after he had been on a bender, Chad came home in a rage. He chased me out of the trailer and into the driveway, and when I tripped and fell, he kicked me in the face with his steel-toed boot. The devastating blow knocked out two of my front teeth and broke a tiny bone in my face.

Crying hysterically on my hands and knees, I dug through the bloody gravel in the dark to find my teeth. Once I had them in my hand, I begged Chad to take me to Jamestown so I could go to the hospital. When we arrived at the ER in the middle of the night, I was obviously traumatized and covered in blood. Chad told the hospital staff that I had fallen, and my teeth were knocked out when I hit the ground. He said he didn't know why I was freaking out and being so dramatic.

Despite my obvious signs of distress, the staff didn't try to get me to tell them the truth about what had happened, but they took his word for it. They reinserted my teeth and had Chad take me to the office of an emergency on-call dentist to put on temporary braces. There was no follow-up, and no one asked what the real story was. They just went about their business, showed very little compassion, and treated me like I deserved the situation I had gotten myself into.

On the exterior, I looked like a strung-out drug addict with a messy life. The staff at the hospital would have to open a whole can of worms to help me out of the complicated situation I was in, and it was easier for them to give me the emergency care I needed and send me back into the trauma and stress that had become my life.

LIGHTBULB MOMENT

 **A lack of training about domestic violence and human trafficking for medical staff caused many victims to fall through the cracks over the years, but we can change that story today by learning the TRUTH about trafficking.**

My Independence Day

During the year I was living in that trailer, I tried to escape from Chad many times. Once, I climbed out a window when he had me locked in the house. I went to the road and flagged down someone to help me. The man gave me a ride to a gas station in Clayton, not far from my mother's house. I walked the short distance remaining, and once I arrived, I collapsed on the couch, exhausted. I fell asleep but was awakened to angry words being spat over me by a maniacal man. Shouting and cursing, Chad carried me away from the house, stuffed me into the trunk of his car, and slammed it shut.

I screamed and begged him to let me out of the trunk the entire twenty-minute ride to his house, but he seemed to drive more erratically the louder I shrieked and cried. Once we got there, he dragged me out by my hair and ripped a huge chunk out from the front of my head, causing agonizing pain. When he got me inside the trailer, he beat me, strangled me until he knocked me out, and kept me in his house for several days.

LIGHTBULB MOMENT

Domestic violence and drug addiction are often common denominators in trafficking victims' complicated lives. These types of complex trauma can keep victims like me bound to dangerous mates and prevent us from breaking free from hazardous situations.

Just because I was not being actively bought and sold during this season does not mean I was free from the tangled web of trauma and exploitation. I thought I would never be able to get away from this violent, dangerous man, but luckily, I finally found an opportunity and leaped at the chance to break free.

On the Fourth of July the summer I was nineteen, I saw my fleeting moment to escape again. We were at Chad's friend's house doing lines of cocaine, and I acted like I was going to the bathroom. Instead, I ran out the back door and down the dirt road, not looking back even once.

I kept running until I reached the highway, and I walked until a man stopped to offer me a ride. I asked him to take me to a nearby town where I knew Billy and my mother were. The bikers gathered to have a BBQ at this park every Independence Day.

When I arrived, several people asked me what had happened to me. It was obvious I had bruises of different colors and various stages of healing all over my body, and I was still wearing the temporary braces on my teeth. I had left my beat-up car at Chad's, but I was finally free, and I went back to stay at my mother's house again that night.

Over the holiday weekend, I went to a small neighborhood bar in Clayton. The bartender served me alcohol despite my being underage. I was young and petite, plus I had braces on my teeth, so I looked more like a thirteen-year-old. At the bar that night, I met a man who promised me he was going to give me a life like I could only dream of. In reality, I ended up in the worst nightmare imaginable.

Chapter 9

ALL MY DREAMS ARE COMING TRUE
Exploitation by Addiction

19 years old

The bar was dim and smoky, and most of the patrons were older men in rugged jeans and t-shirts, their bellies up to the bar with their boots or worn tennis shoes resting along the rung inches above the floor. The men didn't seem interested in much besides nursing their beers and whiskey drinks, but when I walked in, many of them took notice.

I wasn't 21 yet, so I was not old enough to even be in that room, and certainly not old enough to order a drink, but the bartender didn't seem to care. It was better for business to have a young, cute girl shooting pool and keeping the men drinking, so he happily poured me a vodka and cranberry drink, propping a little slice of lime on the edge of the glass.

As I was messing around on the pool table, a man wearing a black leather jacket walked in. He looked my way from across the room, and I instantly caught his attention. He came over and asked me if he could buy me a drink, telling me his name was Damon. When he brought back the glowing ruby-red glass of elixir, he challenged me to a game of pool.

Damon quickly ran the table, and I laughed at how slick he had been, calling him a shark.

He didn't waste any time asking me if I would rather get high than hang out in this dump. I was much more interested in drugs than alcohol, so he paid his tab, and we walked across the gravel parking lot to his car.

Runnin' Down a Dream

Damon drove a silver Corvette Stingray with dark, tinted windows and T-tops. Once he revved up the engine a couple of times, he cranked the radio and blasted rock-n-roll through the upgraded speaker system.

He spun out of the lot, speeding down the road to cut through town, then turned down a road that led us to the country. Damon had a cup filled with booze and ice in the console holder and passed it to me, encouraging me to drink up. It was full of Jack Daniels whiskey, and I gagged down a pungent gulp. I didn't complain, but I preferred sweet, fruity drinks, not whiskey on the rocks.

Before long, the liquor had my head spinning too fast to try to defend myself. Damon sped through the back country roads, and I swirled until I passed out.

The next morning, I woke up sore and confused, seeing the tops of trees swaying above the glass over my head. I was in the front seat of the Corvette with the black leather coat draped over me like a blanket. My mouth tasted bitter, and the light hurt my eyes. I looked over at the driver's seat and saw my new friend Damon waking up next to me.

He offered to take me to breakfast at a diner in Jamestown, and we sat in a booth with our sunglasses on in the restaurant. We nursed cups of black coffee and doused our food in hot sauce in an attempt to kill our hangovers. Over our meal, Damon told me his father had been killed in a tragic accident, and losing him was the hardest thing he had ever experienced. He shared that he had recovered a large amount of money from an insurance settlement after his father was killed. "If you are gonna be my girl, you'll never need to worry about money again. I will take care of you, and you'll have everything you ever want."

His promises sounded *too good to be true*, but as I watched him open his wallet to pay the bill, I noticed it was stuffed full of cash. He left an extra big tip for the waitress, and as we were leaving, he bought some sweet pastries to go. Once we were back in his car, he asked if I wanted to meet the woman he loved more than anyone else in the world. Suddenly, I was worried that maybe he was married and I was a homewrecker. When I voiced my concerns, Damon laughed at me and told me he was single, and I didn't need to worry about him having an old lady. But he said he was taking me to meet an old lady he loved.

Over the River and Through the Woods

When we arrived at his Gramma's house, I quickly saw they had a close connection. She had photos of Damon through the ages all over her house, and there were stacks of clutter—pretty, brand-new things still wrapped in plastic or with price tags attached.

"Gramma, you should use the gifts I bring you. I know you would like them, and I want you to feel loved and appreciated for all you've done for me. Here, we brought you some goodies," Damon said as he handed her the box from the diner.

"You need to stop wasting money on me! I'm just an old woman, and I've made it this long without all these fancy contraptions and designer clothes. I'll keep saving aluminum foil and washing out my plastic baggies to reuse, and you should save your money for starting a family. Who's this little girl? Did you bring her to my house because you want her to be your wife?" Gramma shocked me with her proposition.

I felt my face turning ten shades of red when she mentioned the thought of me marrying this man I had known for less than twenty-four hours, but it did not seem to bother her at all that I was young enough to be Damon's daughter. She led us into the kitchen to join her at the table, pouring cups of coffee with shaking, wrinkled hands before opening the box of sweets to pass around and share.

Gramma asked me a million questions about my life and my family. I shared about my father dying and how I had grown up in a house where I had been pretty much raised by Mr. Earl; how my mother married another man, and I moved out at sixteen to live with my boyfriend; how I had gotten my diploma, and how I guessed I needed to start living like a grown-up.

She wanted to know what was wrong with my teeth that caused me to need braces, and when I looked down in shame, she grabbed my hand and said that I didn't have to tell her if I was embarrassed.

I told her my ex-boyfriend had hurt me, but I didn't want to talk about it. I tried to end the questioning by informing her that the braces should come off next week if I could get a ride from Billy and my mother to Jamestown to see the dentist.

She looked at her grandson and told him sternly that he had better protect me from that monster who had hurt me. Then she instructed Damon to take me to a specific doctor on Monday, declaring she wanted him to pay whatever it would cost to get my teeth fixed. "She is too pretty a girl to have a broken smile. You take care of her; I think she's the one for you!" Gramma made my face turn red all over again.

Leave the Fire Behind—Sparkle and Fade

The next few weeks went by in a whirlwind. Damon took me to his Gramma's dentist and had my teeth fixed, and when we went to see her the next Sunday, she gushed about how pretty my smile was now that my teeth had been released from their cages.

Damon said he didn't want to bring me to sleep in his room at Gramma's, so he convinced me to wait for him to get us an apartment set up in Jamestown. He explained that it took time to have new carpet installed, fresh paint on the walls, and furniture delivered. I didn't mind being patient and waiting for him to take care of all the details.

In the meantime, we made a little pallet of blankets and pillows on the floor of the living room of Billy and my mother's house. It was a temporary situation, but because he was generous with sharing his pot and cocaine with them, my parents had no qualms about a grown man in his thirties sleeping on the floor with their teen daughter and four other even younger girls under the same roof.

With no job, responsibilities, or purpose in life, all I had to do with my time was wait for Damon to come home and pick me up after his workday ended. Every night over those few weeks, he picked me up around 5:00 p.m., and we developed a routine. Once I got in his car, Damon drove to the backroads and parked in a remote area. We settled in, he poured some whiskey into his cup, and he brought out a little metal tube.

The tube had a crusty, wadded-up piece of metal stuffed in one end, and Damon had a small stick he used to shove that make-shift filter back and forth. He took a little baggie of tiny stones that looked like odd-shaped pills and broke them into chunks to spread across the crusty tip. Standing the tube up and lifting it to his lips, he used a lighter to melt the pills, and once they soaked into the crunchy metal filter, smoke came out the other end, filling up our lungs.

The smoke didn't taste like cigarettes or pot but was pungent and powerful. It made my body tingle and relax all over, from the top of my head all the way down to the tips of my toes.

Once we finished melting those pills in the tube, I felt like I was in a dream. When we were getting high, Damon talked to me cryptically, telling me I was beautiful. His words made me feel as high as the drugs we did together. Sometimes I felt like I was hypnotized and intoxicated by his words, even when we weren't melting pills in his car on a dark back road.

The routine he engaged in made it seem like we had been together forever from the very start. Thoughts of Damon consumed me all day, every day. By 4:00 each afternoon, I started pacing and watching out the front door, waiting for his silver car to pull up, eager for our smoke sessions in the woods on the edge of town. Over the two- or three-week period, I became obsessed with him, and throughout the day, I was preoccupied with thoughts of the pills we were melting in the little metal tube.

Movin' On Up

One night, Damon picked me up, and we headed to Jamestown to meet up with some of his friends. He had arranged for us to party in one of the furnished apartments at the complex we were going to move into.

That night, Damon had an eight-ball of cocaine, about the size to fill my fist. He stood over a pan of water heating on the stove and used a baby food jar and some baking soda to turn it from white powder to sticky golden clumps. He balled it up like a chunk of fresh butter, and then broke it up into pieces that looked just like the pills we had been melting in the tubes every night.

As Damon and his buddy Derek huddled in the kitchen cooking the drugs, Derek's girlfriend Julie sat in the living room with me. She acted nervous and spoke to me in a low voice. In an awkward conversation, Julie broke the news that when we were passing around the tube in his car every night, Damon and I had been smoking crack cocaine. I tried to argue with her, telling her it was crumbled-up pills, but she was adamant that Damon had introduced me to crack and "turned me out."

Julie whispered to me that Damon had done this to her, too. He had gotten her hooked on these drugs, and then he "sold" her to Derek. She told me how her life was better than before because she knew Derek would always make sure she had food and shelter for her two young children, whose dads were both in prison. Julie was my age, but Derek and Damon were both in their thirties.

We smoked the entire ball of freebase cocaine that night. If I wasn't already addicted, I was hooked by the end of the night. After Julie and Derek left, I lay in the bed next to Damon and thought I was having a heart attack. I couldn't close my eyes and stared at the ceiling, praying over and over, "God, if there is a God, please save me and help me make it through this night. I don't want to die; I want to live. Please don't let me die. I promise, if you save me, I'll live for you."

The next morning, Damon had a big surprise to show me. We walked across the parking lot, and he turned a key in the door to an apartment facing the hill behind the complex. Inside, there was the beautiful unit he had been telling me about, with brand-new carpet, fresh paint, and gleaming furniture.

Damon had laid out everything perfectly, including a big-screen TV, leather couches, and high-end appliances. I almost cried when we went into the bedroom and I saw the massive king-sized bed, matching dresser, and nightstands. Damon had given me a real bedroom and a real place to call home, and he promised to give me a wonderful life.

We moved in, and he took me shopping to get everything I wanted to fill the kitchen cabinets. We picked out big, fluffy towels and rugs for the bathrooms. It felt like there couldn't possibly be anything better, and everything around us was sparkling and new, full of promise. It was like playing house with an unlimited budget, and Damon included me to give me a sense of ownership and create a deep bond that kept me connected to him and this place.

It might have seemed like the perfect life, but when the drugs started wearing off, it reminded me of when Mr. Earl had moved us into the brand-new house near the junior high school. Things were not as neat and clean as they appeared, and my life quickly went from bright and shiny to dark and defiled.

LIGHTBULB MOMENT

 **Traffickers often present expensive gifts or flash lots of cash in the grooming process, giving the illusion of a life of ease and creating a bond with the victim.**

Carpet Sweeping and Window Peeking

Not long after we moved into our new apartment, several men came by on a Saturday morning. Once the door was closed and locked behind them, they made sure the blinds were closed. After securing the room, they pulled several large Ziplock bags of white chunky powder from their backpacks. They also unloaded boxes of baggies, razor blades, and a couple of digital glass scales.

Damon was in his element working in the kitchen. He cooked up batches of the powder and dumped the fist-sized rocks onto a pretty platter I had picked out on our shopping spree. Once he dropped the crack on the platter, the men busted up the slabs into tiny pieces about the size of a pencil eraser. They sat at our breakfast bar and weighed each of the $50 rocks on their scales before they tied them off in the corners of the plastic sandwich baggies.

This scenario filled me with fear that I could not control. At first, I freaked out so much that the men scooped up piles of the crumbly drugs and dumped them onto a dinner plate for me to smoke. They wanted to make sure I had a never-ending supply, so I kept smoking the whole time they were there. If I ever stopped smoking, I started tweaking and looking out of the blinds, saying we were all going to jail if the cops knocked on the door; so, they made sure to keep stacking up my plateful of crumbled rocks.

When Damon finished all the cooking and the men were done weighing their product, they left a generous amount of drugs for Damon and me to smoke, sell, or share. We tried to ration the dope and usually had enough to last until they returned with a new supply every few days.

Sometimes the men brought wrapped kilos that looked like bricks, and it would take a long time for Damon to cook. He would call Derek and Julie to come help, but Julie and I hung out and smoked in the other room while our boyfriends worked with the other men in the kitchen.

Sometimes between the marathon cooking sessions, Damon and I smoked our entire supply of dope. If all of our calls to dealers for delivery went unanswered, we cruised through Jamestown, visiting the worst places in the underbelly of our city.

These crack houses were filled with desperate, strung-out people who seemed powerless to break free from the grips of addiction. Because I walked in with Damon, I was relatively safe, despite the dangers of those dens of darkness. The overseers of the houses usually showed us favor and gave us more dope than we paid for, encouraging us to stay and hang out. People acted sketchy, picking at invisible specks, and some of them had sores on their arms and faces. As much as I wanted to keep getting high, I hated being in those scary places. I especially hated the way the men looked at me.

Whenever possible, we got our drugs "to go" and took them back to our nice, comfortable, well-decorated apartment on the other side of town.

Just a Burden in My Hand

After several weeks of our kitchen being the cook room for most of the illicit drugs circulating through our relatively small community, things shifted in our relationship. One time when we ran out of dope, Damon said he didn't want to go to an ATM to withdraw cash. He called one of the dealers to bring us some drugs. When the man with the drugs arrived at our apartment, I felt like he and Damon were ganging up on me to manipulate me into doing something I didn't want to do.

It was a trick; it was never what I wanted, but I felt like I was trapped and didn't have a choice.

"He really thinks you're pretty," Damon told me. "And I won't be mad at you. Actually, I'll be really proud of you for earning us some money. And you know he'll give us plenty to smoke if you do a good job. Just go into the bedroom with him and pretend you're in there with me." Damon was persuasive, convincing me to believe it was our best option. I had been conditioned to consume the drug every day for months, and if I didn't get high, I would start getting sick.

At first, Damon even went into the bedroom with us to help me feel more comfortable. I listened to his voice giving me directions in the dark. When everything was over, the shame and guilt felt like they would crush me. There wasn't a big enough pile of rocks a man could leave on my pretty tray; it would never be enough to erase the evil feelings that washed over me. *My body was a commodity*, only good for getting my needs met.

LIGHTBULB MOMENT

Traffickers may orchestrate events so their victims feel trapped in the circumstances. The victims might believe the position they are in is a result of their choices, but the traffickers coordinated things behind the scenes to manipulate and trick them.

My heart grew cold during that season. I no longer communicated with my family and had no contact with anyone who wasn't part of the drug culture I had become entrenched in. My only friend was Julie, and I only saw her when the men cooked the crack in our kitchen. The only people I saw besides Damon, Derek, and Julie were the men who came to our apartment, the people at the drug houses, or Damon's Gramma.

Thoughts and imaginations of abuse tortured me, and I felt helpless to prevent them from hijacking my mind. The only thing that canceled my painful fears and quieted my paranoid thoughts was more of the dope that was killing me. Over those months, I lost a lot of weight, and my body became feeble. I had zero healthy habits and went days without food, sleep, or bathing—only wanting to smoke freebase and stay high.

Damon had created a monster, and he knew the drugs he constantly fed me would keep me completely under his control.

Looking back, it's easy to see how the culture of the illegal drug trade and the world of human trafficking are often heavily overlaid on one another. The crack houses we frequented were always filled with girls so desperate that they would do anything for more money or more dope. The drug dealers knew they could make money exploiting those vulnerabilities, and they alerted pimps and traffickers when potential new victims showed up.

The act of being involved in the illicit underworld of the drug-dealing lifestyle broke down my boundaries and helped traffickers dig in and take control. Dependence and desperation were powerful tools that traffickers used to manipulate me into doing things I would never have considered unless I was under the influence. The guilt and shame that piled up on me as I spiraled deeper into addiction helped them isolate me, keeping me out of touch with family, friends, or other safety networks. I was depressed and started slipping away as I felt my life fading into the darkness.

Picked Me Up and Carried Me Away

This life had been spiraling out of control for about a year, and I didn't think I could survive much longer. After a chance encounter at a gas station, I was connected with my Aunt Donna, my father's sister. She hadn't had contact with me since before my father died when I was five, and my mother had kept her out of my life, never mentioning her to me.

As we began talking and forming a relationship, Aunt Donna made me feel comfortable enough to tell her about the destructive lifestyle Damon had drawn me into. The more I learned that I could trust her, the easier it was to create a heart connection. I was able to let down my guard with her and found the courage to share my fears of being addicted to smoking cocaine.

One day, she came to the apartment and picked me up, literally carrying my small, bony frame past Damon and out the front door before placing me in her car.

That's when I went to live with her brother, my Uncle Joe, for a short time to try to rebuild my life. It wasn't easy to come off the drugs after a year of smoking freebase cocaine nearly every single day, but after a painful struggle, I finally broke free from the dangerous addiction that had nearly taken my life.

Thoughts of Damon never crossed my mind again. He had zero value in my life, and there was not a single day when I missed him or wished we were back together. In my eyes, he was the devil. He had taken me further into the darkness than I ever wanted to go and caused me deep physical and psychological pain. I had no love or concern for him and hoped I would never see him again.

I was only twenty years old and had no skills or resources, but I found out that waiting tables and working at bars could bring me fast cash.

One day, I was working a private catering gig for my boss's wealthy client when I was approached by a guest who introduced himself to me as a club manager named Danny. He went overboard, charming me and telling me I shouldn't be getting my pretty hands dirty serving food. He seemed sweet and obviously had lots of money and good taste because he was wearing fine clothes and expensive-looking jewelry. Plus, everyone at the party knew him.

Before he left, Danny invited me to apply for a job as a cocktail waitress at his popular local strip club. He promised I would make more than twice what I was making now, which almost sounded *too good to be true*. I was intrigued, so I took his card and told him I would come see him at the club. It was hard to tell if he wanted me to call him because he wanted to be my boyfriend or because he wanted to give me a job—or both.

The last thing I was interested in was finding a boyfriend to provide for my needs. Instead, I planned on making stacks of cash like Danny had promised me. Maybe I could save up enough to buy a car and hit the road. I always wanted to explore the country, and if I saved up enough, I could travel wherever I wanted, sleeping in my car along the way.

I was naive and thought working at the strip club would mean living by my own rules. I thought I could find safety in a setting where I'd have a manager and bouncers, and I'd be the one taking the money from the men. I thought I could use my body, which had been sexualized since I was six years old, to make money so I could survive.

I missed all of the red flags Danny was waving, and I didn't have solid boundaries. If I were able to see behind the scenes, I would have realized these clubs often operate in a predatory manner. Managers like him openly recruit young, vulnerable women just to put us on display and up for sale. They work hard to erode any hesitation because the more cash a girl generates, the bigger cut the club can take.

The whole business plan of these clubs hinges on rating women and assigning them a monetary value based on their "assets" or according to their lack of boundaries. A demand-driven succession of porn-addicted, misogynistic men pays for attention, entertainment, and sexual release at the expense of broken girls like me—abuse survivors who have a history of exploitation.

If I had known better, I would have realized I was about to cross an invisible line to enter the industry of commercial sexual exploitation, and all of my mental limits were about to dissolve. But I didn't see the danger ahead, and I called Danny to set up a time to check out his club.

That's when things went from bad to much, much worse.

Chapter 10

STRIP CLUBS AND STILETTOS
Entering the Industry of Commercial Sexual Exploitation

20 years old

The House of Dolls club was about a two-mile walk from my friend Tori's house, where I had gotten ready for my interview with Danny. The weather was pleasant, so I didn't mind walking, but I hoped I would make enough money working at the strip club to buy another car. When I walked up to the front of the club, I remembered going with Mr. Earl to drop my mother off at work.

As soon as I arrived, Danny took me on a tour and introduced me to some of the employees and customers. The atmosphere at House of Dolls seemed electric, with music so loud the bass thumped my chest, vibrating my entire body. Neon lights swirled and flashed around the stage, and an alluring woman in sky-high heels and a tiny thong was spinning around the pole in the center of the catwalk.

Several plush, velvet chairs lined the stage, and others were clustered around small tables throughout the club. A wispy curtain in the corner appeared to lead to another room, with a large man leaning up against the wall next to the entryway.

Several dancers dressed in sexy outfits were scattered throughout the place, either at the bar or at various tables. Danny introduced me to a cocktail waitress and the bartender, and I was a little surprised to see they were not wearing much more than the dancers.

All in the Family

As we made our way through the club, Danny introduced me to a dark-haired dancer who was sitting with Johnny Rocket, one of his regular customers. "Call me J.R.," the man told me, taking my hand in his and raising it to his lips to apply a delicate kiss.

J.R. bought me a drink and asked me a lot of questions: Was I in school? Did I have a boyfriend? What kind of car did I drive? He was surprised to hear I didn't have a car and said if I needed a ride to work, he would be happy to pick me up for my shift and take me home every night when my shift was over. He also insisted I let him drive me home from my interview, saying it would be unsafe for me to walk home after all these men in the club had gotten a look at me. Both Danny and the pretty girl sitting with J.R. agreed, telling me it would be best for J.R. to take me, so I decided to let him give me a ride back home.

Before he walked away, Danny told me to be back the following day to work my first shift and instructed me to wear an outfit and shoes like the other waitresses had on. "You can expect to make some good tips tomorrow!" he said as he left me in J.R.'s care.

"Welcome to the family!" the bouncy young dancer cooed at me, batting her eyes and flashing a warm smile.

J.R. ordered another round of drinks, and the three of us toasted to my new job at The House of Dolls. Once I sucked down my frozen pink beverage, J.R. and I said goodbye to the girl at his table, and he handed her $20 as we stood up to leave. I could hardly believe that he had paid her just to sit there and drink with us.

Who's Gonna Drive You Home Tonight?

When we got to the front door, J.R. handed the valet $10, and the young man sprinted across the parking lot to fetch a sporty, baby blue Jaguar convertible. As my body sank into the rich, buttery leather seats, my driver sped off onto the street.

Maybe it was the alcohol, or maybe because my nerves had been so on edge while we were at the club, but for some reason, I was out of my element, and it took a few minutes to realize I had not told J.R. where my uncle lived. I asked him if he knew where he was going, and he told me he had to stop at his house to pick something up before he ran me home, but it would only take a minute. "You don't mind, do you? I promise I'll be quick!" he said as he turned into a private community, hitting a button on his visor to open the big metal gate.

"Oh sure, no problem," I mumbled, starting to feel just a tiny bit anxious that maybe I shouldn't have accepted a ride from a stranger. I did have a little consolation knowing Danny and all of the people at the club seemed to know and like him, so I quickly dismissed my thoughts of concern.

When we pulled up to his place, I was amazed to see a lavish mansion with an expansive oval driveway. J.R. drove right up to the massive double doors at the front of the house. Once he put the car in park, he came around to open my door like a perfect gentleman.

When we were inside, I tried not to let my jaw drop too far to the floor. I had been in fancy houses and country clubs before, but this place was like what you see in the movies. The rooms were huge, and marble floors stretched in every direction, with perfectly placed designer furniture and stunning crystal chandeliers everywhere I looked. Enormous art hung from the walls, and a set of glass French doors led to a patio built around a sparkling pool surrounded by lush landscaping.

A Barbie Girl Living in a Barbie World

My new friend led me out to the patio, where I saw a beautiful blonde woman swimming in the pool. J.R. waved at her and called her over to us. She came dripping out of the water wearing a skimpy bikini and grabbed a towel to dry her curly hair as she walked over to where we stood.

"This is our newest family member over at House of Dolls," J.R. proudly announced.

"Hi, I'm Barbie. I work at House of Dolls, too!" she bubbled.

When I introduced myself, she asked, "Is that your real name?" I told her that, indeed, it was, and she and J.R. both acted surprised. Barbie told me I needed to come up with a stage name because I didn't want people to know my real name. She and J.R. were adamant it would be dangerous to let anyone associated with the club know my real name, especially the customers, since they can be dangerous and unpredictable. They assured me that a stage name would offer me a sense of protection. Not sure what she meant, I told her I didn't know what a stage name was or how I would pick one.

"It's easy," she said. "Just think of something you like that everyone would associate with you. Like, my name is Barbie because everyone always told me I look just like a Barbie, and now I work at House of Dolls, so it was the perfect name!" She giggled a silly laugh, and I understood why that name fit her so well.

"In that case, I think maybe I could go by Harley," I said, thinking of all the times I rode on motorcycles and hung out with bikers growing up. Both of them agreed it would be the perfect name for me, with J.R. joking about how he couldn't wait to take a ride on his new Harley.

LIGHTBULB MOMENT

 **Strippers and other people working in the commercial sex industry often protect their privacy by using a pseudonym as a marketing gimmick to separate them from the character they play or the person they become as their bodies are commodified.**

J.R. told Barbie, "Harley is going to need a new wardrobe to get started as a cocktail girl, but we expect she will be dancing soon. I want you to take her to get some outfits and shoes for work. Go ahead and take the Jag." He leaned over, kissed her on the cheek, and handed her a credit card.

"OK, Daddy, no problemo!" Barbie chirped, flashing a huge smile.

I was shocked that J.R. would tell this woman to take me shopping when I had only met him a little more than an hour earlier. But Barbie wasn't surprised at all. She led me back into the house, and we went into one of the bedrooms, where she told me to have a seat while she got ready. I sat on the luxurious linens spread across the big brass bed and watched in awe as she stood in the elegant ensuite bathroom and blew her hair dry. She walked into the closet and emerged wearing a pretty pink sundress and sandals. "Let me grab my lipstick and then we'll go," she said, her eyes sparkling.

The rest of the day felt like a dream, and Barbie took me to a couple of shops like I had never seen before. The only clothes and shoes these places sold were the types the dancers and waitresses wore at the strip club, and they almost seemed more like costumes than actual outfits. These stores didn't sell anything normal women would wear in public.

Barbie and I became fast friends. I learned she was only a couple of years older than I was, but she was a real pro at the business of entertaining men. She picked out the perfect outfits for me and helped me adjust my straps or zip up my dresses, overflowing with compliments about how great each ensemble looked. I felt totally at ease with her. When I saw the totals at the cash registers, I was shocked, but she whipped out the credit card and told me not to worry about money anymore.

"J.R. and Danny want you to feel sexy and beautiful! You're a good investment, and I'm sure you'll be worth every penny," she said, a smile beaming from her face. Barbie knew best, after all.

When we were done shopping, I told Barbie I should probably be getting home so my uncle wouldn't worry about me, but she convinced me to wait and call him when we got back to the house. "I really hope you won't run off. We have plenty of room, and I don't mind sharing anything to help you feel more comfortable," she cooed.

Once we returned to the mansion, we dropped our shopping bags in her room, and we went into the kitchen to discover J.R. had spread food and sparkling wine out on the granite island. He and Barbie greeted one another with a passionate kiss, which made me feel a little embarrassed, like I was invading their personal space.

Anxious to call my uncle, I asked J.R. if I could borrow his phone. He gestured to where the phone was hanging on the wall, but before I could dial, he grabbed my hand and told me Barbie wanted me to spend the night so we could get ready for work together the next morning. "Yes! That would be perfect!" she exclaimed, jumping up and down and clapping like a giddy schoolgirl.

"Just tell your uncle you're staying with friends, and I promise I'll drop you off after your shift tomorrow," J.R. said.

I felt even more awkward thinking about spending the night in a strange place with people I had just met, but Barbie handed me a glass of champagne and toasted me, clinking her glass with mine. "Here's to our first slumber party!" she smiled. "Like I said, we have plenty of room, and I will help you do your hair and makeup before work tomorrow. It will be so fun," she said, batting her big, blue eyes at me.

"Well, OK, I guess I could use some help getting ready. The girls at the club were wearing a lot more makeup than I am used to." I took a sip of the sweet sparkling wine and agreed to the sleepover, then ducked around the corner to make my quick call. When I came back into the kitchen, Barbie was sitting on J.R.'s lap, feeding him a juicy strawberry. He motioned for me to come closer to them and rubbed my arm up and down. "We noticed you seem a little anxious. Barbie has something that could help you relax," he mentioned.

My Own Prison

"Have you ever done ecstasy?" she asked me, her pretty eyes flashing behind her silky lashes. I told her I had heard of it before but had never done it. "Oh, you'll love it! It's better than champagne and will help you to feel really good, inside and out. Let's split one and go get in the pool; I love swimming under the stars as it starts kicking in!" Barbie twirled a tiny pastel pill between her manicured nails and used a paring knife to cut it in two.

"Just let it melt on your tongue, and while it's starting to work, we can go get into our bathing suits," she told me as she popped the pill into my mouth. Grabbing my hand, she led me across to her bedroom, asking J.R. to put some music on for us as she pulled out a basket overflowing with skimpy bikinis.

When we went out to the pool, the low techno beats were already thumping through my body, and once we dipped into the water, I understood why Barbie liked it so much. The water seemed to open up to receive me, and I wore it on my body like a cloak. As I started swimming, the world spread out in layers, swirling around me like a symphony. I could hardly believe that just half of a tiny little pill made me feel so different, so alive, so connected to the world.

I never expected the things that happened throughout that day or night to be my reality, but in a blur, I ended up staying with J.R. and Barbie for an extended time. It was easy for me to fall out of contact with my newly-found family and isolate myself from them as I fell deeper into the trap of the drugs and wild lifestyle. As my addiction progressed, I came into a rhythm of partying and working. I was soon spending all of my time with Barbie and J.R., and everything happened in a very natural way. It was an easy transition for me to go from an abused little girl to a teenager whose boyfriends beat me, tricked me, trapped me, and turned me out, now into an unsuspecting young woman sharing a sugar daddy with a stripper.

Don't Want to Come Down from this Cloud

The ecstasy pills made me feel wonderful when we took them, but the coming down was brutal. As the drug wore off, it caused me to swirl into a tunnel of despair, and I felt as deep in the darkness as the euphoria took me into the light when I was high. Coming down made my body ache, and I wanted to sleep for days, but I had to work at the club. As much as I wanted to get high every day, J.R. and Barbie said we were only allowed to do it at the house, never at work.

One night, when Barbie and I didn't have to work the next day, J.R. took us dancing at a techno nightclub. That night, Barbie and I each took a whole pill, which gave us the energy to dance all night long, for hours on end, barely taking breaks. She showed me how to dance like the girls at the club, and we used J.R. to practice our moves. When we started coming down from the drugs, Barbie had other pills she shared with me—some that took us up and others that took us down.

I may have started working as a waitress at House of Dolls, but it wasn't long before the regular customers, J.R., and Danny convinced me to take the stage for the amateur costume competition on Halloween. Barbie helped me decide to dress up as a Playboy bunny, complete with a cotton-tail and tall, pink ears.

As I was getting ready to show off my costume, I remembered when Mr. Earl and my mother would have me search for the hidden bunny on Hugh Hefner's magazine covers when I was a little girl. I always thought the ladies in the pictures were so glamorous and beautiful, but now I wondered if they felt like I did inside. After a few weeks of working in the club and staying with J.R. and Barbie, I had gotten strung out on drugs again. I could barely remember what it was like to live a normal life.

I was nervous about being in the spotlight and feeling the judgment of everyone's critical eyes, but as she helped me with my hair and makeup, Barbie slipped me a small piece of an ecstasy pill. That helped me relax so I could turn on my sex appeal. She also gave me a little pep talk and told me I would do great, telling me to remember what we had practiced.

Can You Take Me Higher?

As the drug started kicking in, it was time to get in line and join the procession of other first-timers and dance across the stage to show off our costumes. Right before I walked up the stairs, I had a flashback to the beach bikini contests my mother put me in at ten and eleven years old. I remembered what it was like when I was a little girl, on stage with the grown women who were most likely strippers, and those memories gave me the confidence I needed to get up there and strut around in my bunny suit.

The DJ put on a classic rock song and announced, "And here is everyone's favorite cotton-tailed cocktail waitress, Haaaarrrr-ley! This little bunny might just be a young thing, but she will get your motors running, boys!"

I strode across the stage to whistles and shouts from the sea of men filling up the room, and as I spun around in my bunny suit, my long hair swayed across my back. The crowd was cheering me on, and I grabbed the pole in the center of the stage to twirl around a few times. It all felt very natural and easy, and I realized I loved the attention I was getting from all of the men. Suddenly, my high heel slipped, and I looked down as I caught my balance, shocked to see the stage was being covered with money! I had awkwardly spun around a few times but barely even tried any dance moves, so I wasn't expecting tips.

When my turn to dance was over, Barbie helped me gather up all of the cash that had been thrown on the stage, and we waited off to the side as the last few ladies did their dances. Then all of us amateurs went back up on the stage for the DJ to announce the winner. I was genuinely shocked to hear my name called for first place, and I could hardly believe I won $500 for less than five minutes on the stage. After I received my prize, J.R., Barbie, and I celebrated with champagne.

They told me they were proud of me, and J.R. asked me if I would like to double my money and make another $500. I didn't know what he meant, so I asked him how I could do that. He told me it was simple; it was time for me to stop being an amateur. He said I needed to accept my fate and see what the crowd was demanding. That was the night I would become a real, professional dancer instead of just being a cocktail girl. J.R. said he would be my first official customer for a private dance in the champagne room.

It was an easy decision.

Promise Not to Stop When I Say When

Once we were back in the private room, it was just the two of us because Barbie had stayed behind with the others at his table. Girls were dancing for their customers throughout the room, and a big bouncer was standing by the door, but J.R. and I were off in a corner with billowy curtains separating us from full view. The waitress brought us a bottle of champagne, and when J.R. paid, he told her that we wanted privacy—the extra tip he gave her was for her to stay away.

After drinking some bubbly and dancing to a few songs, it seemed like J.R. changed how he treated me, but I did what Barbie and I had practiced. When we were finished in the back, I went out into the main club where Barbie had already lined up men to buy champagne room private dances with me. That night was my first taste of the real financial impact that could be gained by stripping, and I became as addicted to making easy money as I had become hooked on the designer drugs.

I finally lived the life I thought I wanted—staying in a beautiful home, driving fancy cars, and wearing nice clothes. But the truth was, I was empty, broken, and desperate for a healthy life. It took a lot of drugs to stay numb enough to live that lifestyle. Maybe it looked glamorous on the outside, but that's how traffickers dress things up. In actuality, it was a dark time, resulting in another season where I had little contact with my sisters or anyone else in my family. I was becoming isolated again.

After the night of the costume contest, when I started dancing at House of Dolls instead of cocktail waitressing, I began feeling strung out from all the pills. I didn't want to be in that type of lifestyle again. The drugs and the wild situation with J.R. and Barbie were too much for me to handle.

I told J.R. I was going to move in with my friend Tori, who was going through a divorce and needed a roommate to help pay the bills. He was angry, but he had become interested in another new girl at the club. It was tough to say goodbye to Barbie, but I moved on, happy that I never saw them again.

Free-Fallin'

After I moved in with my friend Tori, I tried working a legitimate job at a Tex-Mex restaurant in the suburbs, but that didn't last long. I was hooked on the cash and the culture of the strip clubs, so I applied for a job at a club called Centerfolds.

At the club, after I filled out the application, Josh, the manager, took a copy of my driver's license and told me to be back at 7 p.m. to work my first shift. Again, *my body was a commodity*, and it was only good to get my needs met.

Not long after I started dancing at Centerfolds, Josh asked me, "Do you have any other friends with daddy issues? Y'all make the best strippers," as he laughed a crude laugh. His joke wasn't funny.

The sad truth is that I was not an anomaly; that is how many of the girls I worked with in the strip clubs ended up there. Many of us were victims of childhood sexual abuse, and most of us had daddy issues. None of us woke up one day and chose that path. We may have been convinced that it was our only choice—or it may have been our last choice—but if given another choice, I don't think any of us would have stayed in that lifestyle.

Girls, Girls, Girls

Contrary to popular public narratives about strip clubs being empowering places where women can make stacks of cash, experience taught me it was easy to get into the industry but very difficult to get out. Many women involved in the industry are sexual abuse and assault survivors, and many became involved in commercial sex while minors or right after coming of age. To understand how the sex industry operates, we can look at data as we ask some critical questions.

- Why do strip clubs often advertise with words like *girls, barely legal,* or *amateur night*?
- Why have porn sites historically reported that popular searches on their platforms include terms like *teen, college,* and *innocent*?
- Why do porn sites host videos of child sexual abuse material (formerly referred to as *child porn*), resulting in over 36 million reports last year?[1]
- If adult businesses like porn sites make money from those videos through memberships and/or ad revenue, are they complicit in child sex trafficking?[2]
- Why does the subculture involved in this industry have such an influence within our society today, especially with the entertainment influencers that many young people follow and idolize?

- Why would a teen magazine promote content about the commercial sex industry in a positive light if its target audience is focused on minors?[3]

- Why does the sex industry promote "amateurs" instead of professionals with experience and tenure? Is this proof that they seek vulnerable people who are least able to protect and defend themselves?

- Does the exploitative system indicate that strip clubs are trafficking inside a building and pornography is trafficking on camera?

Stripped of Dignity

Strip clubs are built on the business of selling access to someone's body. It seems like the owners and managers want the women working for them to remain in a state of dependence so they can continue with their selfish pursuits of money-making or fantasy-fulfilling. Desperate women are more likely to do whatever it takes to make ends meet, so these traffickers and buyers will continue to push boundaries and strip away objections to get all guards to come down.

This stripping away usually doesn't happen all at once but is often a gradual decline down what becomes quite a slippery slope.

An example of women's dignity being stripped away is during the coronavirus pandemic, when a popular gentlemen's club in the Dallas-Fort Worth community was advertising with the phrase, "Support Single Moms," on a banner hung in front of their business. This gave the illusion that they and their customers were giving poor, desperate women a hand up to help them prosper and thrive, but that is the last thing those buyers and sellers desired.

A customer bringing stacks of cash to a strip club to support single moms is the furthest thing from a charitable action. Charity is donating groceries to a food pantry, but these women working at the club had to perform to receive the support. Contrary to the marketing campaign the strip club used, buying a lap dance is not a benevolent act.

It's important to realize that once a woman is put out for display on the strip club stage or in front of a web camera, she will be rated by the men in the crowd, and a price or value is applied for what she's worth.

These men will judge her appearance and decide:

- Is she *worth* buying a drink for and having a private conversation with?
- Is she *worth* buying a table-side lap dance from or subscribing to her private page?
- Is she *worth* a private dance in a booth in the back room of the club or a private meeting on a streaming porn channel?
- Is she *worth* offering an extra tip to do more than dance or for a private request on a porn site?
- Is she *worth* offering even more in exchange for an encounter outside of the club or in real life?

LIGHTBULB MOMENT

Every human has an inherent value and a worth that cannot be defined by dollar signs and decimals, but human traffickers only see the money generated by the exploitation of women displayed in strip clubs, on porn sites, and on street corners.

Paying with My Life

Sadly, after a night filled with dehumanization and being violated by the customers I interacted with throughout the evening, the sweaty, crumpled cash strewn about the club wasn't even mine.

Tipping out the support staff is a common practice for strip clubs. That means a large portion of the cash that I had earned by baring and humiliating myself belonged to the managers, house moms, bouncers, DJs, bartenders, cocktail waitresses, and valets. On top of that were the pimps who ultimately controlled the flow of money in the club. If I didn't pay the right people the right amount, I couldn't ensure my safety while walking to my car at the end of the night with a wad of cash in my bag. Not cashing out the support staff meant I risked the bouncers at the club turning a blind eye if a customer tried to go too far.

Empowered people don't have to make survival-based choices like these.

Strip clubs are just trafficking in a building. I had no more power over my own body in the confines of the strip club than I had as a victim of trafficking on the streets. It was my experience that these clubs are built on the exploitation of vulnerable young women, and the customers use their money to erode any boundaries that a woman working there may try to retain.

The strip clubs I worked in while I was being trafficked often also served as storefronts for drug dealers and pimps who wanted to exploit a market opportunity to profit from their products and grow their illicit businesses. Before long, I found myself caught up in the drug culture of the club and became entangled in a sinister situation that seemed impossible to get out of.

---

[1] National Center for Missing and Exploited Children. "By the Numbers." https://www.missingkids.org/gethelpnow/cybertipline.

[2] Mickelwait, Laila, *Take Down: Inside the Fight to Shut Down Pornhub for Child Abuse, Rape, and Sex Trafficking* (Penguin House, 2024). https://www.penguinrandomhouse.com/books/711836/takedown-by-laila-mickelwait/

[3] McNamara, Brittney, "Cardi B Won't Let You Disrespect Her Because She Used to be a Stripper," Teen Vogue, February 28, 2018, https://www.teenvogue.com/story/cardi-b-wont-let-you-disrespect-her-because-she-used-to-be-a-stripper.

Chapter 11

ROCKSTAR ON THE RUN AGAIN
Cut My Hair and Change My Name

21 years old

Working at Centerfolds turned out to be one of the worst decisions of my life. I was stuck in the vicious cycle of the sex industry, with the only constant thing being the never-ending flow of men willing to pay the price to access my body while I was in that vulnerable state. Because I was a broken, damaged-goods abuse victim with "daddy issues," my only value was the price a man was willing to pay to get a glimpse or grope of my flesh.

At the time, my desperation drove me to show up for my shifts, and by the end of every night, I had less reason to live and more to feel desperate about.

Where Everybody Knows Your Name

After a couple of months of hustling, I finally had some regular customers who came to see me a couple of times a week. Devin, a bearded, dark-haired man who was the boss of the landscaping crew, stopped in often, saying he just wanted someone to talk to. If he brought his employees with him, they usually wanted dances, but Devin just wanted to buy me drinks. We would talk about random things, like the places I dreamed of traveling.

Devin made me feel safe, and he even brought me a cell phone so we could talk when I wasn't working or he wasn't able to come to the club. This was the late 1990s, so having the flip phone in my pocket put me on the cutting edge of technology. I took it as a sign that Devin liked me and wanted to be my boyfriend. When we talked, he said things about us having a life together and spoke into all of my dreams of traveling.

I started fantasizing about spending my days raising babies in a suburban home and cooking meals in a bright, clean kitchen. As the owner of the company, Devin surely would work hard to provide an honest life, and the more we talked, the more I trusted him and could see us having a future.

Sometimes he called me from his truck, and I could hear the lawnmowers and leaf blowers revving up as his crew worked in the sizzling summer heat. But Devin would be as cool as a cucumber sitting in the air-conditioned cab of his pickup truck because he was the boss. He was the big boss, and he was going to build a life for us. I became infatuated with thoughts of us being together.

One night, Devin showed up at the club with a new guy on his crew. He told me he was an old buddy from out of town, then he asked me if I could get them some blow.

"I don't have any, but everyone knows the dude in the blue jacket who sits at the end of the bar will hook you up. Just go ask him," I replied. I definitely didn't want his buddy to leave if he didn't get what he wanted. He might try to convince Devin to move the party to the strip club across the street so he could score some coke. If they left, my tips left with them, and I wouldn't be able to make enough money to pay my rent that was coming due.

Devin responded, "I feel awkward going up to some stranger and asking him to hook me up with some coke. Since the guy already knows you, could you please just get it for us? I'll make sure my buddy buys you a drink and tips you well," he pleaded with me.

"OK, I will go ask him for you. But one of you guys will need to go to the men's room with him to get the package," I said as I got up to walk over to the bar and talk to the man in the blue jacket.

As soon as I told him my regulars wanted to party, he was up and walking to the men's room. Nodding my head, I motioned for Devin to send his friend in behind him. Devin's buddy followed the guy in the blue jacket into the men's room, but when he came out, he kept walking right out the front door without even saying thank you or goodbye.

"What a jerk!" I told Devin. "Didn't he think any of the rest of us would want to party, too? He could have shared some with those of us who have to work through the night," I mumbled.

"Yeah, he's a total coke-head," Devin laughed. "He's probably out in the parking lot snorting lines as long as his arm by now."

"Well, that sucks because I was looking forward to partying a little tonight. I've been a good girl and haven't gotten high for a minute," I told him.

"If that's the case, I'm happy to get you and me some X if you want to take this $40 and go get us some," he told me, passing two $20 bills across the table.

"Really? That's awesome! I'll be right back; don't go anywhere," I told him.

I snuck over to the ecstasy dealer and covertly bought some pills from him, then secretly passed one of the pills to Devin as I melted a candy-colored pill on my tongue. I asked him, "Aren't you going to take that? I thought you wanted to party, too," to which he replied, "No, I can't take it now because I have to drive, but I'll be thinking of you when I pull it out later tonight, don't you worry."

As the pill dissolved in my mouth, I knew it was too late to change my mind or decide to wait until later. After a while, Devin decided they needed to go find his coke-head buddy and head to dinner. As always, he generously tipped me and the other girls at the table. Before he left, Devin thanked me again for hooking them up.

He Came Looking for Me

The next day, the phone Devin had given me stopped working. Foolishly, I never wrote down his number, expecting to be able to hit a button anytime I wanted, and I had no idea where to get a cell phone fixed. Plus, I had decided to move in with a different girlfriend on the opposite side of town, and I tried to work a regular job waiting tables at a Tex-Mex spot.

One night, after I had worked a double shift and was about to clock out to walk the mile to my apartment, I noticed that a man who had been seated in a booth twenty minutes earlier still hadn't been waited on. My overwhelmed coworkers frantically asked for help, and I clocked back in to bring this man a burrito and a beer. He was polite and didn't complain about the long wait or the short staff. After I brought him his check, I realized he was flirting with me, but he didn't overwhelm me with romance like all the creeps from my past. Instead, he asked me out on a date like a proper gentleman.

He told me his name was Robert, he had just moved to town because his boss was expanding the company to our area, and he was a trainer. He was a nice-looking man, with blazing blue eyes, an infectious, sparkling smile, and long, curly hair. He treated me with respect and didn't push me past my boundaries the way I was used to men treating me. Robert was polite and had good manners, and it was immediately evident that he was chivalrous and dignified. He asked me if I would be his date for a concert coming up in a few weeks, and I agreed to consider joining him. After writing his name and phone number on a bar napkin, he drew a little map to his apartment.

I went to that concert with Robert, and we truly had an unbelievable time. Over the weeks and months that followed, I started building a friendship with him, but I was not a healthy person. He wanted to be my boyfriend, but the closer we grew, the more I was overwhelmed with shame. I thought if he knew the truth of what I had been through as a child and a young woman, he wouldn't want to be with me, so I pushed him away instead of running into his arms for safety.

Before long, it was apparent that the tips from waiting tables were not enough for me to live the drug-fueled lifestyle I had been living. The more memories of my childhood would pop up, the stronger the fires of addiction raged. As the drug scene and fast cash from the strip clubs beckoned, my girlfriend and I got jobs at a cabaret strip club near our apartment complex.

In a huge twist, about a month after I started at Cabaret, Devin and one of his workers walked through the door while I was at the club! I was so happy to see him, and he bought me a couple of drinks so we could catch up.

"I thought I was never going to see you again," I told him, sipping my fruity cocktail through the short black straws. "The phone you gave me died, and I didn't have any way to contact you," I said.

"Harley, we probably went to ten different clubs trying to find you," Devin told me. My heart fluttered in my chest, and I interpreted his looking for me as a sign that he wanted to be with me. Devin knew the truth about me—that I was a stripper, and I knew how men wanted me to use my body on their command. I didn't have to feel ashamed around him because he had seen me stripped down to nothing so many times.

We had a great conversation, but as quickly as he had walked through the door, he was gone again. Before he ducked out, Devin promised he would see me again soon, turning to wave goodbye as he left.

Not sure what to think about the situation, and not trying to get my hopes up or my heart broken, I worked the rest of my shift and tried to put him out of my mind.

The next day, I had another shocking surprise at work.

Bad Boys, Bad Boys

As I danced on the stage, a big, fat sheriff's deputy walked through the door. I watched as he talked to the doorman and showed him a piece of paper, and then I saw the doorman point to the stage like he was directing the officer to me.

The cop walked over to the edge of the catwalk, and I bent down to hear what he had to say. He asked me what my full name was, and I told him we don't use those names in this place, but he could call me Harley. He proceeded to tell me he had a warrant for my arrest and that I had to come down from the stage immediately.

I was shocked, and with the music and lights still pumping, it felt like I was drifting away to another planet. I climbed off the stage, and the DJ called up the next dancer to take over. When I asked the deputy what he meant by "a warrant for my arrest," he informed me that he was there to take me into custody.

The deputy asked me if I had some different clothes I could change into since it was cold outside and what I had on was inappropriate to wear in public. He offered to take me to my locker so I could gather my things.

Again, I asked him what the warrant was for, and he told me I would be served with the papers once we were at the processing facility. Firmly, he told me that he needed me to get my things and go. But because I had a small amount of marijuana in my bag, I was not prepared to have a cop watch me go through my locker.

I didn't know what his warrant was for, and I certainly did not want him to know about the illegal weed in my locker, so I fibbed and told him what I was wearing was how I had arrived at work that day. He seemed doubtful that I had driven to the club in a bikini, thigh-high leather boots, and a long black cape, but since I refused to change clothes, he told me to turn around so he could cuff me.

A tangible wave of shame washed over me as the cop snapped on the handcuffs and led me through the club, out the front door, and to his waiting squad car, where he put me in the back seat.

Caught in a Trap, Again

As he drove through town, I started crying, clenching my teeth to stifle my sobs as hot tears ran down my cheeks. With no idea what I had done to get arrested, the longer he drove, the more concerned I became. Instead of driving to the jail facility on the south side of town, this deputy pulled into a basement parking garage under a high-rise building downtown.

Maybe this guy isn't a cop; he never served me that warrant, I thought as my heart pounded in my chest. Worried that I was caught in a scam and concerned he was just pretending to be a cop to get me into cuffs in the backseat of his car, I was afraid of what was going to happen to me. I did not feel safe.

"When am I going to find out what's really going on?" I asked nervously as he pulled up along an elevator.

"Slide over and get out of the car," he commanded as he held the back door open.

The cold air rippled across my exposed skin, and I deeply regretted not getting dressed in clothes that would offer me more protection and dignity. The shame built as I walked alongside the uniformed officer and we stepped into the elevator.

When we arrived on the floor he had selected, we walked down a long hallway with my high-heeled boots click-clack-clicking on the glossy tile floor. It felt like we were in an empty office building, and my skin prickled with goosebumps from the cold air circulating through the space. I had a building fear that something was very wrong with this situation. "Where are we? Why didn't you take me to jail? This isn't right; what the hell is going on here?" I asked in desperation.

"You'll find out soon enough, miss," he answered as he led me into an office with an open door. He told me to sit in a chair at a long table that looked more like a boardroom than a police station. "You sit there and wait, and all your questions will be answered shortly, miss," he said cryptically as he left the room, closing the door behind him.

I was freezing and wished my arms were not cuffed behind my back so I could wrap them around my bare torso or rub my hands up and down over the tingling skin of my icy arms. Minutes ticked by, and I grew colder as my fear mounted.

Tears ran from my eyes, running down my face and dripping into a little puddle. I bent over and lay my head sideways along the table in front of me, trying to alleviate my shoulder tension from being in such an uncomfortable position for so long. The handcuffs were tearing into my wrists, and no matter how I attempted to adjust myself, I could not relieve the discomfort.

I remembered the empty prayers I had prayed while I lay in bed with Damon after smoking an eight-ball of cocaine for the first time, and I started repeating what I said in my mind as I felt my death closing in on my doorstep.

"God, if there is a God, if you are real, please help me. I don't want to die; I don't want this to be the end of my life. Please help me make it through the night," I prayed silently in my heart as the tears continued to flow. These solicitations to an unknown god were ultimately answered, but I wasn't snatched up out of danger and carried away to safety as I hoped.

I Have Become Cumbersome

When the door opened, I sat up and nearly fell out of my chair.

Devin and two of his "employees" strode through the doorway with badges hanging from their necks.

"You didn't have to get all dressed up just for me," he said with a crooked smirk smeared across his bearded face.

"You're a COP?" I asked incredulously as waves of shock and disbelief washed over me. "What is this all about? Why are you guys all wearing badges? Are you a cop?"

"Yes, Harley, we are detectives. I had you brought in here tonight so we could talk to you about the very serious crimes you committed at Centerfolds. We are here to help you figure out a way to get yourself out of this mess of trouble you've gotten yourself into," Devin told me as he stood over me, holding a manila folder in his hand.

"What do you mean by crimes I committed? I never did more than dance for you; I never touched you, but you touched me! You're the one who broke the law!" I screamed, terrified at the revelation that this trap was even worse than I had imagined.

Narrowing his eyes to look at me, Devin responded, "Well, Harley, that would be your word against mine. I am an officer of the law with years of service to the people of this community, and I have the witness testimony of these other detectives as well," he motioned across the table to where his two minions sat. "But you're just a drug-addicted stripper with no purpose in life. You are a pariah to society who offers zero value to the world." His words cut me to the quick. Devin may have been an officer of the law, but to me, he was a bad cop.

Devin ripped into me, asking, "Whose side of the story do you think a judge or jury will believe? Upstanding citizens don't want a girl like you peddling drugs in this town. Remember, Harley, if you have to sit in the witness box to testify, the state's attorney will bring up details about all the men you have been involved with. From what you've shared, your ex-boyfriends all seem to have a long history of crime and incarceration.

"Besides, the cocaine and ecstasy we bought from you have been tagged as evidence. That's all we need to put you behind bars," Devin concluded, sliding the folder across the table so I could see the photos of the tiny pouch of white powder and the pastel pill from that fateful night when his "buddy" from out of town visited the strip club.

Protesting, I exclaimed, "What are you talking about? I never sold any drugs to you! I am not a drug dealer!"

As he leaned over and rubbed my arm with the palm of his hand, Devin told me, "There's no use arguing the facts or crying about your pitiful situation; it's time for you to face the reality of the circumstances you have created for yourself."

Devin tapped the bulging file folder on the table in front of me. "This report is all the proof we need to show the court that you did, indeed, coordinate the sale of illegal substances. And these are serious charges, young lady. Felonies." His voice was deep and brooding.

My heart was thumping in my ears, and I felt my stomach drop to the floor. In my mind, I saw a series of life's events coming together to lead me to this point, starting with when I was a little girl and Mr. Earl and his friends had me dance for them in our suburban living room. I saw Billy, who had me find my inner "Harley," to Mr. Ed and Damon, who had gotten me strung out and pushed past any boundaries I tried to maintain. The word "felonies" echoed in my head. "I can't believe I ended up in a situation like this. I don't know what to do," I sobbed pathetically.

Devin responded, "Harley, this could be the end of your freedom. Unless you agree to help us," he said with a twinkle in his eye.

"Help you? What is that supposed to mean? Help you do what?" I bawled helplessly as hot tears streamed down my face.

"We are prepared to help you make all of this go away," Devin told me with a stern tone. "This file contains felony drug trafficking charges. If you help us collect the evidence that we need to arrest some people we have been watching, we can help you make everything in this folder disappear. Then you can go on with your life as if it never even happened," he said matter-of-factly, not taking into account what this would mean for my safety.

"Oh, you want me to be a snitch?" I asked him incredulously. "I don't think you know what you're even asking; I can't be a snitch." I shook my head in disbelief.

Devin had already put together his plan, and he told me, "Harley, there's a way for you to help yourself out of this mess. We want you to work at BJ's Club on the south side. There are a few men who frequent that club, and they are involved in moving large quantities of dope through our city. All you need to do is befriend them and wear a wire when you make a few small buys. You can trust us to protect you as you gather the evidence, and we will provide the marked money for you to make the purchases. As soon as we have what we need to press charges on these guys, we can have the judge drop these felonies we have you on." He made it sound so easy and looked down at me with a glint in his eyes.

"You don't have to tell us now, Harley. You can think about it for a few days, but you'll be doing your thinking from a cell in the county jail," Devin replied with a heaviness in his voice.

Realizing this was not a situation that would easily go away, I tried to flip the switch in my brain from survival mode to negotiation mode. I stammered, "Wait a minute, tell me again exactly what you want me to do. How can I make you happy so you will help me out?"

Mustering all of my experience in smooth-talking to get men to do what I wanted them to do, I cocked my head to the side and turned my chest toward him. I could only imagine what my haggard face must look like with streaks of mascara smeared all over my red, puffy eyes. It was hard to look alluring or sensual, but I did my best.

"And, please, could you loosen these awful handcuffs? They are cutting into my wrists," I begged as I batted my eyelashes.

A flash of relief crossed Devin's face. "If you're ready to work out a deal, I will absolutely loosen the cuffs. I'll even take them off while we sit here and discuss the details of your opportunity for freedom." He pulled out a set of keys and unlocked the shackles, finally freeing my hands from the torturous devices.

"It's pretty cold in here, and I wasn't dressed to be in an office with the air conditioner on. Do you think you can help me with that, too, please?" I asked as demurely as possible, briskly rubbing my arms to try and chase away the tingly cold.

"Sure, we'll get you a blanket and maybe a cup of coffee; how's that sound?" Devin asked me. I nodded, and he sent one of his men to get me what I needed to warm up.

Outshined

Devin's associate brought me a crappy Styrofoam cup of lukewarm coffee and an oversized sweatshirt. We sat there for about an hour, and my former knight in shining armor showed me photos and information about some of the men they would like me to befriend and eventually make purchases from. I put on a great act, pretending to be on board with their diabolical plan, but looking at the mugshots of the hardened criminals they wanted to pit me against made my skin crawl.

"Look, Devin, I'm sure I can get these biker dudes to trust me. After all, my name is Harley," I joked, getting a laugh from the trio. "But it might take time, so let's talk about how quickly you expect all of this to take place?" I asked hesitantly.

"I think six to eight weeks should be enough time to complete a couple of buys, but we can see how it goes and get an extension if needed," my new boss said.

"OK, if we are going to do this thing, let's do it. I'll go to BJ's tomorrow and get everything set up right away. Are you going to give me a ride home now? And maybe swing by a drive-thru on the way? I'm starving," I said lightheartedly, hoping to get another chuckle from Devin and his guys.

The men looked at one another and then down at the floor.

Devin tried to appear compassionate, replying, "Harley, I'm sorry, but it will not be possible for you to return home tonight. Because of the magnitude of the charges leveled against you, we are required to take you to the county facility where you will be processed and booked. However, because you agreed to help us with the case at BJ's, you will only have to spend one night in custody. We will have a special release coordinated for you sometime tomorrow. Don't worry, we won't leave you stuck in there all weekend."

I broke down in tears again, trying my best not to give up hope or let on that I was just telling them what they all wanted to hear. "Does that mean you're going to put me back in cuffs again?" I sobbed, my head in my hands.

"Unfortunately, we will need to cuff you again, but I'll stop on the way to get you a burger, and we can wait until after you eat to put them back on. Once you get to the holding tank, they will take them off again," Devin told me as he stood up and signaled to his men that it was time to get moving.

Fly High, Free Bird

Devin kept his end of the bargain. That night, on the way to the jail facility, we stopped at a fast-food joint before he put the cuffs on me again. The next afternoon, I was released from the county jail on a special bond.

I did not keep my end of the bargain.

The offer the officers made me was no bargain but was another deceptive ploy from yet another trafficker. Devin was a shady cop, and I was being exploited by these detectives. They wanted me to put myself in an extremely dangerous situation, building a case involving violent criminals and drug dealers, to help advance their criminal justice careers.

Using money from a sugar daddy I had met while dancing at Centerfolds, I found an attorney who said he could help me. I tried to fight the charges, but the crooked lawyer seemed to have never-ending legal bills. After a while, his running tab grew to the point where I couldn't keep up, and the attorney fired me as a client. Since he was no longer retained as my legal counsel, no one made court appearances on my behalf.

That meant there was another warrant for my arrest, and this time not just for the drug trafficking felonies, but the judge stacked on additional charges of failure to appear and obstruction of justice as well.

I was desperate to avoid being locked up again and would have done anything to evade being put behind bars. At the same time, I didn't want to have to outrun angry drug dealers from biker gangs who were infamous for making people disappear. In my distress, I decided that running from the law was the only viable option I had at the time.

Before long, I was on the run again. But I wasn't a twelve-year-old little girl anymore. I was a desperate, grown woman full-throttle in survival mode. I was a product of the abuse I experienced at the hands of my mother, Mr. Earl, and all the others who had exploited me and broken me down. The only thing I had going for me was the skill and fortitude I had developed to know how to talk men into helping me out in exchange for what they wanted. My life as a runaway played on repeat again.

I cut and dyed my hair, got a fake ID, and headed south, hoping to discover a way out of the colossal mess I'd found myself in. There was no way I could have known how terrible my situation was about to become. I had already lived through child abuse, drug overdoses, and violent beatings, but the road in front of me held unspeakable horrors like I never could have imagined.

Chapter 12

THIS IS REAL PIMPIN'
Truck Stops, Street Corners, and Motel Hell

23 years old

My life running from the authorities spanned a few years, and I became extremely resourceful at finding ways to make enough money to have food and shelter. I continually watched over my shoulder, remaining fearful of getting picked up by the police again. This caused me constant paranoia, which drove me to find the drugs I needed to silence the echoes of danger and keep my anxiety in check.

When the occasion arose, I would work shifts in strip clubs, but I had to be choosy about where I danced. If the wrong person were to find out I was using a fake name, they could either turn me in to law enforcement or they could turn me into their slave, so I was very selective about where I worked.

My survival skills were crucial, and I traveled from state to state often to keep a low profile. Over the years, I stayed in touch with Robert on and off, and he was one of the few people who knew my real name and about the cases I was running from. Spending a few weeks with him was always refreshing because I could let my guard down. But I could never get comfortable for too long, and I'd be off and running again.

The situation was exhausting, and I was in perpetual survival mode. Not only did I have to avoid being captured, but I didn't want to end up sleeping under bridges and digging food from trash cans again, so I did whatever I had to do to avoid the fate that loomed over me like an ominous, dark cloud. When I didn't think things could get any worse, a series of circumstances led me into a devastating predicament that only a miracle could get me out of.

Goin' Off the Rails on a Crazy Train

Over the years of my life on the run, I had few friends besides Robert, but I found new sugar daddies. These were older men with illicit enterprises, so they had enough money to keep their wives happy at home with plenty left over to help me get by, too.

A few years into my stint on the lam, I was staying in motels and trailer parks in Florida. I did my best to hop from couch to couch or from room to room until I overstayed my welcome. One day, a motel manager banged on the door of my room one minute past check-out time. He demanded I clear the room for him to sell it to the next guest, but I had nowhere to go. I begged him to give me more time so I could formulate a plan of action for where I would hide out next.

I usually could come up with the cash to keep myself in a room for a week at a time, but the sneaky strings of addiction kept dragging me back down to the pit of hell. When I became mixed up with the drug scene in Florida, I was swept into the toxic world of smoking speedballs, and the mix of cocaine and heroin had a tight grip on my life.

In my desperation, I called Robert, whom I hadn't spoken to for some time. I pleaded with him to wire me some money under my false name so I could pay the motel bill for another week. He knew about the legal cases hanging over my head, but he didn't know how deep I had fallen into addiction until I called him in distress.

At this time, Robert lived in the mountains of western Arkansas, and instead of agreeing to send money, he offered me a reprieve from the streets of Tampa, where we both knew I wouldn't be able to survive. In spite of my frantic state, he was honest, calm, and kind, and he even made me laugh, so I was able to let down my guard and agree to accept his lifeline. I knew he was a genuinely nice guy I could trust. He sent me a bus ticket so I could stay at his place to get clean while I put my life together.

This man was unlike any friend I'd ever had before. From the first time we met several years earlier, Robert let me know he had feelings for me that were more than just friendly, but I could never see myself being his girlfriend. Over the years, I had met his parents and the son he had with his ex-wife, and I knew he came from a great family. Plus, he was running a legitimate business, he had a house in the mountains with a spectacular view, and a lot of things were going well for him.

I, on the other hand, was a total train wreck. I thought if Robert ended up in a relationship with me, I would probably ruin everything he was working so hard to build. I was damaged goods, and I had thoroughly shattered my own life. I didn't want to destroy his, too. Now I was detoxing and would be sick for days or weeks, and he would have to take care of me as I sweated it out.

Despite my reservations, I accepted Robert's offer for an emergency ticket to Arkansas. Once I gathered the few items I had in the motel room, I made my way to the bus station and settled in for a journey west, excited to reconnect with my good friend and feeling a glimmer of hope that I could get back on the right track.

Down in a Hole, Losin' My Soul

I made it the first leg of the journey with my shoulder up against the cold window of the rambling bus. I slept off and on through the afternoon and into the night. Now, the sun was up, and I was feeling the effects of the drugs leaving my system. Dope-sickness can be an overwhelming mix of nausea, sweats, vomiting, paranoia, exhaustion, convulsions, and hallucinations. Public transportation was not the ideal setting for those symptoms to kick in.

Knowing that once I got to Robert's place in Arkansas, I would have to go cold turkey off the dope, I wanted one last high. When my bus stopped for an afternoon layover in Memphis, I decided to call Big E, a dope dealer I knew from the area. I asked him if he could come to pick me up so I could smoke for a couple of hours. Big E was happy to hear from me and told me he would head that way and see me soon.

My craving for the substances had driven me to put myself into a situation worse than anything I could have imagined; if I'd had a glimpse of what was about to happen, I would have run away and never turned back. But my body was already reeling from withdrawals, and the aches and cramps made me desperate to get high again. I could hardly wait for my dealer to pull up in front of the station.

Big E arrived with his rap music turned up and windows rolled down. As soon as I got in the car, I had a surge of cravings for dope. Luckily, I had just enough cash to get a supply that would last me the rest of the trip across Arkansas. Then, once I arrived at Robert's house, I planned to toss my glass pipe and suffer my way through the detox, sweating it out on his couch.

But I wasn't ready to quit just yet.

I wanted one last chance to say goodbye to getting high.

Big E told me he had his stash out at the farm, and we hit the highway to an exit about twenty minutes north of the city. My body was twitching from withdrawal, and I reminded him I had to get back to the station before my bus left. He told me not to worry; he would make sure I got where I needed to go. I had my transfer connection ticket wrapped around my fake ID in my back pocket, but other than that, all of my worldly belongings were in a backpack on his floorboard between my feet.

We went down the back roads into a place I never would have been able to find without a map and some detailed directions. As Big E pulled up in front of a broken-down house with boarded-up windows, I handed him my cash, and he ran inside to fulfill my dope order. Realizing how far away from the bus station we had driven, I was increasingly uncomfortable waiting in the car for him to come back. With each minute that ticked by, I became more worried that we wouldn't make it back downtown in time for me to catch my connection.

When Big E finally came back out, he tossed a tiny baggie of dope in my lap. Seeing the drugs made me crave them even more, and I could hardly contain myself as I waited for him to drive away from the boarded-up shack to a place where I could get high.

As Big E backed out of the driveway, I told him, "Thanks, man, I really appreciate you hooking me up like this, but after I smoke this dope, we need to get back to the city so I don't miss my bus." I tried to sound lighthearted and carefree, but I had an ominous feeling that things were about to go from bad to worse. I didn't want to miss my ride to Robert's.

Big E drove down a dirt road to a desolate place and pulled into a field that was surrounded by a grove of trees that lined the street. Behind the wooded fortress, we were virtually hidden from view. "I know you can't wait to get high, Harley. Go ahead and smoke out," he said, a Cheshire Cat grin spreading across his face. He stepped out and leaned against the car as I excitedly tore into the package and prepared to have my personal out-of-body experience.

As soon as the dope hit my system, I faded back into the seat and felt myself floating away to outer space. It was all I could do to keep the pipe in my hand and not burn my leg or singe the upholstery in Big E's car, but I held on long enough to load up a second hit. That was the one that sent me to the moon. I didn't pass out, but I did check out of reality for a little while.

After several minutes, the drugs started to wear off, and the world was coming back into focus. Looking around to get my bearings, I was horrified to see several cars had pulled up in the secluded little grove. A crowd of young men milled around Big E's car, looking at me through the open window, making catcalls, and saying disgusting things about me. They were dressed like gangsters, and some of them had bandanas tied around their mouths to disguise or obscure their faces. One of the men opened the car door and tried to drag me out, but I climbed over the seat, desperately trying to get away from him.

The crowd erupted in shouts, telling him, "Get her! Get that b———!" as the attacker climbed into the backseat, crushing himself on top of me while he yanked off my clothes. He covered my mouth with his forearm, so I couldn't scream or cry, but I did all I could to push him off of me, trying to bite his arm and fighting with all I had to try and stop his assault.

The whole time I wrestled against the thug, rap music blasted loudly from a set of speakers, and the crowd roared. The man was much bigger and stronger than I, and he was driven by a dark, demonic force. My fight against him was to no avail, and it soon became apparent that he wasn't the only one who had come to that secluded place to have their way with a woman who wouldn't be able to defend herself. Every man there took a turn assaulting me, and by the second or third thrashing, I shut down and became completely numb.

I had gone from fight mode to zombie mode.

All Been Washed in Black

In my mind, I went to a place where I had gone many times when I was being abused as a child. My imagination allowed me to put a type of shield up to guard me from the reality I was experiencing, and the storyline I saw playing out in my dream-like state involved a hero coming to save me, chasing the bad guys away.

Eventually, they left, and Big E tossed a rag back to me, telling me to clean myself up and get dressed, and he was going to take me back to town. When I crawled out of the backseat and returned to my spot next to him up front, I broke down crying when I saw my glass pipe and baggie of dope had been crushed and shattered, smashed into the floorboard. I had hoped to get at least one more hit before we drove off, but now that was not an option.

Big E drove down the dirt roads back out to the highway, his music blasting so loud that the bass thumped my chest. I rested my weary head along the door, letting the wind whip across my tender face. My whole being ached, both from the attacks and from the dope wearing off all over again. Silent tears dripped from my eyes, and I felt an immense weight of sadness and hopelessness. Physical ripples of pain traced up and down my body in waves, but emotionally, I felt empty and distant from reality.

Once we were on the highway headed toward the city, I mustered up a tiny fragment of hope that within a few hours, I would be with my friend Robert in his mountain-top home on the other side of Arkansas, but when Big E took an exit to go east instead of to the bus station downtown, my hopes were crushed again. He pulled off the highway and parked in front of an apartment building, gruffly instructing me to get my things and follow him.

When we went inside, I was sad to see a young woman sitting up against the wall, looking at the floor with her shoulders hunched like she had been disciplined or punished. A shirtless man came from the back room and told me to have a seat, then told Big E to follow him into the room he had come out of. I sat against the wall next to the girl, who was careful not to look directly at me. I could tell she wanted to communicate with me somehow, but the atmosphere in the place was dismal.

After a few minutes, the door opened, and the two men emerged. Big E walked right out of the door without even looking my way, leaving me there on the floor at the shirtless man's feet, clutching my backpack in my arms. "You need a shower, go get yourself cleaned up, then we are going to work. You gotta earn some money back for me, b——," he said with a thick southern drawl. Tugging at my arm, he had me stand up and pushed me toward the open bathroom door.

I was numb and felt like I was floating above my body, watching myself take a shower and wash my bruised flesh. I dug my cleanest clothes out of my backpack and tried to make myself look as presentable as I could. I figured by "going to work," the man meant heading to the strip club, and I did my best to put on some makeup and brush the tangles from my hair.

Not My Time to Wonder Why

I was wrong about the strip club, though. When I went back to the living room, the man told the girl sitting against the wall to get up and get ready because she was going to show me the ropes. She jumped up and went to the bathroom and came out a little while later, wearing a beautiful wig of long, silky black hair and a tiny, tight dress with stiletto heels.

As we left the apartment, I felt like I was walking through the middle of a bad dream. My voice had been snatched right out of my mouth, and everything felt like it was melting around me in slow motion.

I followed the man and the girl with the long wig as we walked across the parking lot to a black SUV. The man got behind the wheel, and the girl climbed into the front passenger seat. As my hand reached out to open the car door behind her, I saw a flash across my mind of the backseat of Big E's car, and my entire body froze. The man opened the window and started yelling and cursing at me, telling the girl to get me into the vehicle. She jumped out and opened my door, pushing me to get in, saying under her breath, "You better act right. Please don't make him mad; just do what he says, and we will be OK."

As we left the property, the driver angled his rearview mirror so he could see me and told me we were going to the truck stop. "You ever worked the lot before?" he asked me, a deranged look flashing across his eyes.

I looked toward the mirror and shook my head back and forth. "You ain't say much, do you?" he asked. Again, I shook my head back and forth, but I didn't hold his gaze for long. There was something sinister driving him, and I felt like whatever demons were oozing through him would transfer into me if I stared into his depraved eyes.

Run Through the Wicked Garden

We headed to the busy truck stop along the interstate highway. Once he pulled into the parking lot, our driver backed into a parking space where he had a full view of the line of trucks and sternly told us to get out and not come back until we had our quota.

We exited the vehicle and stood on the asphalt next to the SUV so the girl could adjust her wig in the window's reflection. Orange overhead lights cast an eerie luminescence around the lot, and several trucks were idling, causing a low rumble to echo across the expanse. The air smelled like diesel fuel, pitch, and metal, and some of the trucks glowed with auxiliary lights down the sides and below the cabs. My new partner started walking toward one of the gleaming vehicles that had its engine running. "You just follow my lead; I'll do all the talking and negotiations, OK?" she asked me, looking for confirmation that I understood before she put her hand on the arm of the mirror sticking out to the side of the driver's door of the semi cab. After climbing up the two metal stairs, she knocked on the window, and after no answer, she knocked again. A bearded man rolled down the window and shouted, "Get outta here, ya little hussies! Stay away from my truck! I'll call the law and report you—get on outta here!"

As she scooted back down the steps, she pointed out a sticker at the bottom of the door and told me, "I shoulda known he wouldn't make a good customer. See this?" The sticker was a cartoon of an iguana in a dress with a blonde curly wig and lipstick. A big red circle was drawn around the reptile, with a line slashed through it diagonally. Big letters read, "NO LOT LIZARDS!"

"Girl, we gotta meet our quota so we can get back home," my partner said, headed to the next truck that had its low lights on and engine rumbling.

This time, the man was happy to see her on the other side of the window and motioned for her to go around to the opposite side. She opened the passenger door and climbed up in the cab, then looked down at me and said, "Get in, silly!" as she laughed and tossed her hair back flirtatiously. I followed her up into the truck, and she reached over to pull the big, heavy door closed behind me.

I had never been inside a truck like this before and was surprised at how large everything was with all the dials and gadgets across the dashboard. The seat was big enough for both of us to squish in and sit together, and I was shocked to see that behind the seats was a little bed dressed with a blanket and pillows and tiny twinkling lights dangling from the ceiling. It was almost like a camper inside a car, and I suddenly realized the man probably had us climb up into his truck so he could get us onto that bed with him. A wave of terror washed over me, and I felt my stomach drop to my feet.

"What you lookin' for, mister?" my partner asked him, tossing her hair and putting on a sexy act. He told her, graphically, exactly what he wanted, and she gave him a dollar figure in response. "Is that for just you or both y'all?" he countered, looking the two of us up and down with his hungry eyes.

"That's just me tonight, sweetie. She ain't broke in yet; I'm just showing her the ropes tonight. But she can watch if you want her to; would that be alright?" The girl was a tough negotiator.

"OK, but next time I expect a two-for-one special!" he laughed, showing stained teeth behind his curling lip as he ducked back to the bed. She followed him into the tiny room and started to pull a curtain across to offer privacy, but he protested the barricade. "You said she was gonna watch; how's she supposed to learn if she can't see what you're doing?"

he objected. Pulling the curtain open to expose the space, she looked at me pitifully and whispered, "Sorry," then turned her attention to her customer.

I didn't watch but instead stared down at my feet, wishing I were anywhere else in the world at that moment. I remembered times in motel rooms in Tampa when my roommates had brought men back to our room, and I would sit in the corner chair or on the other bed while they conducted business like this. I didn't want to be in this terrible situation, but I had no way to stop it from being my reality.

The girl didn't take long to finish the job and collect the money, and when she came back up front, she ushered me out the door, tugging at her dress and straightening her wig before heading over to the next potential customer. She got turned down at the window again, and off we went to the next truck in the row.

She became more bubbly and chatty the longer we walked, and she asked me a bunch of questions, but I was still mute and couldn't even remember what my voice sounded like. During her ramblings, she mentioned something about only being fourteen years old, and that gave me a pain in my chest like I had been stabbed in the heart.

She was so tiny that I should have assumed she was young, but I never expected her to be a little girl who was barely out of junior high. She babbled about how she had won the favor of the man she called Daddy, how he had bought her this dress and wig, and how he promised they would go shopping again soon. She said she thought I had what it took to keep Daddy happy if I could just learn how to talk to these men and get their money.

LIGHTBULB MOMENT

 **To traffickers, truck stops are like fishing in a stocked pond for buyers. Truck drivers are often lonely and looking for human connection, plus many of them have a sleeping area in the cab and disposable income from their well-paying jobs.**

Taste the Pain

The night dragged on, but as the sun started to come up, we headed back to where Daddy was parked and got back into the SUV. He had been asleep with his driver's seat leaning back, but when we got in, he sat up and put out his hand, demanding the money from my new friend. She handed over a stack of cash, and he counted it, then looked at her with angry eyes. "This is only half! I told you to show her the ropes. Where's the rest of my money?" he screamed at her, his face on fire.

"Daddy, I did all the work tonight. This girl is so green she can't even say a word. Maybe tomorrow she'll be ready, but she just can't do it yet. Something musta happened to make her clam up. Maybe she needs some food and sleep to get adjusted or something," she responded, trying to calm him down. I broke out into a sweat and felt waves of fear washing over me, coupled with the guilt of knowing it was my fault she was getting in trouble.

"OK, b—, we will get you straightened out when we get back to the crib," he said, looking at me savagely in the rearview mirror as he pulled out of the parking lot. We drove back in ominous silence, and the sun was starting to hurt my eyes as it lit up the world.

When we returned to the apartment, my new friend took off her wig and quickly fell asleep on the couch. While she slept, Daddy had me follow him to his bedroom. He had me sit on the bed and stood in front of me, staring at me with a sinister vibe, and then he started talking to me in strange riddles.

He told me he was building an empire, and I could be one of the bricks. If I showed him that I was solid, I could be a building block in the castle he was erecting. He said I had what it took if I would just open my mouth and talk to these tricks; he had put good money into me, so I needed to catch the game quickly and turn him a profit. None of the words he said made much sense to me.

Trying to get me to let down my guard, Daddy turned on some low R&B music. He coaxed me to lie back, and he came over and started pulling my clothes off. I turned stone cold and stiff again, and I just stared at my bag lying on the floor across the room.

After he tossed my clothes to the corner by my backpack, Daddy backhanded me across the face and said, "Hoe, don't you ever go out in the field and not bring me back my money!"

My face throbbed where his hand had struck me, but I continued to stare at my clothes in a pile next to my backpack on the floor. I couldn't find the strength to fight or even try to push him off of me, and I just kept my gaze on my bag and my clothes as tears started flowing from my eyes.

As I lay motionless, Daddy wrapped his hand around my throat and started to choke me. I had a memory wash over me of Chad strangling me at his trailer, and I started to fade away into the darkness.

Run Like Hell

Suddenly, the door to the room burst open, shattering a set of glass shelves with a loud crash as a frantic situation unfolded. A giant man in a dark blue uniform stood in the now-open doorway. He was shouting, Daddy was shouting, and their words were mixing with the screams of the girl in the other room.

The man in the blue uniform had both hands wrapped around a large gun that was pointed in our direction. Daddy jumped to his feet and put up his hands, yelling and cursing at the man with the gun. It was chaotic and confusing, and I was terrified.

In all the mayhem, I rolled off the bed, grabbed my clothes, and pulled them on in record time. The man with the gun kept shouting, the girl in the other room was screaming at the top of her lungs, and Daddy kept his hands up, yelling back at the gun-wielding intruder.

When I saw my chance to escape, I grabbed my bag off the floor and sprinted out of the room, squeezing past the uniform-clad giant to run into the living room and through the front door. I ran out into the bright daylight, breathing heavily to fill my lungs with air as I sprinted along the row of apartment buildings to a fence at the edge. I quickly climbed over the chain link and ran through the woods behind the complex.

My body surged with energy, and adrenaline coursed through my veins, propelling me to flee the dangerous situation. As I darted through the wooded area, my arms and legs were sliced by little thorns and thistles, but I didn't slow down. My bare feet kept moving, squishing through the mud and dirt to get away from the scary men in that bedroom.

I ran as fast as I could, searching the woods for a path to follow through the trees. I was terrified that one of the men was following me. After splashing quite a distance through the mud while my legs were being slivered by sharp, spiky bushes, I saw I was finally at the edge of the thicket.

My wounded feet began to ache a little more with each passing moment as I stood at the edge of the path. I scanned the forest's meandering boundary and crouched down as I made my way through the crunchy leaves at the edge of the trees. I was barefoot and covered with mud and bloody scrapes on my arms and legs.

When I found a gap in the foliage, I exited the woods into the wide open. Taking a deep breath, I stepped onto the dusty sidewalk and felt the cool concrete under my mud-encrusted toes.

Walking in Memphis

I felt a wave of familiarity with the sensation of escaping, and a memory of running away at twelve years old flashed through my mind. Being on the run was a common theme in my life for over a decade, and I knew that I needed to come up with a plan, or I would be sleeping under a bridge again.

I crossed the street and made my way to a set of brick-and-concrete apartment buildings, hoping to find a place where I could figure out a way to get back to the bus station and make it to my friend Robert. Thoughts of sitting next to him on the front porch of his mountain-top home gave me hope to find a way out of this impossible situation.

Just as I stepped my bare feet out into the oil-stained lot, a dark red Cadillac pulled right in front of me and stopped, separating me from the brick buildings. The passenger window lowered, and sitting in the leather driver's seat was a dark-skinned man dressed in a silky purple shirt with his hand dangling across the steering wheel. He asked me why I was standing outside barefoot and offered to take me to get cleaned up and get some shoes.

That man took me to a dive motel where he let me take a shower and wash the mud and blood off my legs and arms. He gave me a bag with some clothes and shoes in it and told me that he was putting me out on the track. He also showed me a bag of dope and told me that it would be my reward at the end of the night.

LIGHTBULB MOMENT

 **Potent drugs like cocaine and heroin are powerful tools that pimps use to control their victims.**

The man barked at me, frantically stomping his feet and waving his arms, screaming about getting his money. Once he opened the door, he grabbed me by the shoulder and shoved me outside, demanding I put myself out on the street. My voice had vanished, leaving me betrayed and unable to defend myself.

I walked out to the street and saw several other scantily clad women and girls walking up and down the sidewalks as cars cruised by. Just like when I was sleeping under the bridge when I was twelve years old, cars would pull next to a curb or turn into a parking lot, and a girl would lean into the window before getting into the passenger seat and riding off with the man behind the wheel.

This was the last situation I ever wanted to be in. I knew some girls in Tampa who frequented street corners and motels like these to get fast cash so they could score more dope, but I had tried to stay away from those areas. I never thought I would engage in street prostitution like that. It was the lowest point of my entire life.

At the end of the night, I failed at the assignment the man had given me. I was a horrible prostitute. My fear was paralyzing, and since I couldn't muster a word or negotiate, I didn't bring much cash back to my pimp at the end of my terrifying time on the track.

Give It Away Now

The next day, I found myself in the backseat of the Cadillac with the man in the purple shirt driving me through a neighborhood. He made a call on his cell phone, and I heard his half of a conversation with someone on the other end of the line. "Yo, man, I got this little white girl who ain't make me any money. She's green as can be, and I ain't got time to mess with her. You wanna take her off my hands for $250?"

I instantly felt devoid of any value. I knew he was talking about me, and he was talking about selling me for $250. The thoughts that bubbled up in my head were as crazy as the conversation I was overhearing.

I'm worth more than $250! I thought to myself. *If they took me to get some nice clothes and makeup or picked a better hotel where they gave me shampoo to wash my hair, I could be worth more than just $250!*

I wanted to show the driver I was worth more than the price tag he was placing on me, but I knew I looked like trash, and my face and body were covered with swollen bruises and scrapes.

Much to my surprise, shortly after his phone call, the man drove up in front of the bus station where I had phoned Big E just a few days prior. He pulled up to the curb and told me to get my bag and get out. I assumed the person he was talking to told him to just dump me out, and I was so grateful he had returned me to a place where I could continue my journey to get to my generous friend Robert, who was only one state away.

I grabbed my backpack and exited the vehicle as quickly as I could. As soon as the door was shut, the driver sped off, mumbling something about me being too stupid to do what he needed me to do.

It would have been best for me to head to Arkansas and hide out at Robert's place, but my body was beaten and bruised, and I was still in survival mode after all of the trauma I had endured. I didn't want my friend to see me like that. Plus, my brain was still tangled with the cords of addiction.

At that moment, I was no longer being controlled and sold by maniacal pimps, but I was still captive to my dependence on the illicit substances. I had become a full-blown junkie, and these pimps were holding baggies of dope over my head like rewards. I was dying from the dope and the addiction.

Chapter 13

CAN'T FIND MY WAY HOME
Left Me Far Behind

24 years old

Looking back on that day, I know it was nothing short of a miracle that the man left me on the curb in front of the bus station. I can't imagine what the other people in the establishment must have thought of my pathetic existence.

Not only was I dressed inappropriately for such a public place, but my body and face were covered with bruises, and my arms and legs were sliced with little cuts from my run through the thorn bushes in the woods.

I went into the bathroom and cleaned myself up at the sink before digging out my clothes from my backpack. I put on a big hooded sweatshirt and a pair of long pants that concealed me from judgmental eyes. I was grateful for the shoes I had been given by the pimp the night before, happy that I wasn't barefoot at the bus station.

Before I stuffed my dirty clothes into the bag, I pulled out my fake ID and my canceled connection ticket.

Scar Tissue

My body and heart were broken, and I was bruised from head to toe. Over the past several days, I had experienced compounded trauma in a capacity that I had never gone through before. I hadn't been the same since I had traveled out into the country to get some dope with Big E.

When I looked in the bathroom mirror, I realized I couldn't go to my friend Robert in the state I was in. I did not want him to see me like that, and I was afraid I would destroy all the great things he was building for himself.

When I had last seen him, I'd stayed at his place for a while, and we'd had a few wonderful weeks together. He had taken me to church because he said he wanted to find some positive people for me to hang out with. His mother raised him to have a good, healthy life and contribute something constructive to society, and he was an honest and honorable man. I felt now that if I showed up on his doorstep in the condition I was in, I would just drag him down into my filthy pit.

After mulling over my options, I decided to use the pay phone and made a collect call to one of my sugar daddies. When he answered the phone, I realized that I quickly had to find my voice.

Whispering and hoarse, I told him I was stranded in Memphis and had been hurt, and I begged him to send me money so I could get a bus to my grandma's. He told me this was the last time he would bail me out, but he would wire the money in the name of my fake ID. With my gravelly voice, I thanked him and told him I would do my best to repay him someday. He laughed and told me to get my life together and to stop wallowing in the gutter, then he hung up.

As soon as the money came through the transfer, I purchased a new ticket to Jamestown and bought some food from the cafeteria-style counter at the station. Once I had my ticket and some food in my belly, I found a place on a long bench to wait for my scheduled ride.

Every bone in my body was aching, and my heart felt like it was melting away to nothing. I had become numb and felt emptier than I had been when I arrived at the station less than a week earlier. I was afraid I was about to tunnel down the spiral of destruction again.

This Is Not My Beautiful House

I got on the bus and rode the long trek back to Jamestown. My plan to keep my head down and look as unfriendly as possible worked, and no one bothered me or said so much as a word to me on the trip.

When I called my grandma to let her know I had returned to the area, she sent my grandpa to pick me up and bring me to Clayton. My grandpa was shocked to see the state I was in, but I told him I had been jumped by some girls who tried to take my bag, and I had put up a fight. I held up my ragged backpack like a trophy to show him I had the victory. "You should see the others," I joked, my bruised face aching as I cracked a crooked smile.

At my grandma's, it was a little harder to look her in the eyes and lie about how I ended up looking and smelling like I did. I told her the made-up tale about being jumped, but I could tell she didn't buy it.

As usual, she spoke sweetly and seemed understanding as she took my bag of rotten, reeking laundry and sent me to shower. She turned on the washing machine and got to work preparing a meal for my grandpa and me.

After half an hour or so, I emerged from the bathroom with my hair shampooed and conditioned, my face clean and shiny, and sweet-smelling lotion rubbed all over my pitiful body. Grandma set a giant plate of steaming homemade food before me, telling me to eat before it got cold.

I cried as I bowed my head, thanking her for cooking for me and thanking the invisible God, whom I still wasn't sure I believed in, for bringing me back from the pit of hell.

That evening in the guest bedroom, I climbed into a soft, fluffy bed with too many overstuffed pillows in a room filled with delicate, collectible knick-knacks, dainty doilies, and Victorian antique furniture and lamps. The shiny floral wallpaper wrapped around the walls was sporadically broken up by ornately framed prints of little girls in ruffled pinafores, playing with kittens or sitting at a gleaming piano. From nearly every conceivable angle, porcelain dolls with pretty, pale petticoats under their patterned dresses smiled at me with their perfectly painted pink lips.

My grandma had already washed my bag of dirty laundry, and it was either hanging in the closet or folded in a neat little stack on a bench by the door. The room smelled like flowers and soft-scented soap, and the billowing layers of lace curtains fluttered in the breeze of the rotating fan as it swirled the air around the tiny space. It was such a stark contrast to the world I was in just twenty-four hours earlier, and I was never happier to be at the only place my heart had ever called home.

The safety and security of that bed, the fully stocked refrigerator I could open and raid on a whim, the spotless bathroom filled with powders, perfumes, and fluffy white towels—it almost seemed like too much. I felt like it was being wasted on me, and I would never be able to belong in that home after the evil I had committed.

As the night drew darker outside the window by my head, the memories of what I had experienced in Memphis started to emerge like a picture show in my mind. I felt powerless to do anything to stop the film reel that was looping in my mind, showing graphic scenes of the rape, abuse, and exploitation that I had endured.

Cut Ties with All the Lies

The faces of every man who climbed on top of me in the back of Big E's car, the pimps who had smacked me and strangled me and sent me to the truck stop parking lot and street corner in front of the motel, the men who slowed down to judge if I was worth the fee they would have to fork over to get me alone long enough to do what their hearts and minds had conceived. All of those faces flashed through my mind.

Just the remembrance of such evil acts seemed to desecrate the meticulously decorated space in my grandma's guest room, and a thick, dark evil hung heavy over my head as I lay on the ruffled bed.

My face and body throbbed where every swollen bruise left tangible reminders of the result of my choice to make that call to Big E to score some dope. I had chosen to get in the car with him. I wanted to get high more than I wanted to make it to my friend Robert, who loved me so much that he sent me a lifeline when I was begging for help from Florida.

I had been at rock bottom in Tampa, and the grip the dope had on me had scared me to the point that I thought if I didn't find a way to escape, I was going to end up dead behind a dumpster. Maybe that was the fate I should have allowed to unfold, because I certainly didn't deserve another chance at life after all the damage I had done.

I didn't deserve a friend like Robert, who sent me a ticket out of a dead-end situation. I didn't deserve a cookie-baking grandma who made the bed cozy for me with extra layers of ruffles, and I certainly didn't deserve to be in a safe, warm place far away from the reality of my depraved and desperate choices. Yet here I was, casting a dark shadow in an otherwise lovely place. I was going to ruin this guest bedroom just like I ruined everything else I had ever touched with my defiled, dirty hands.

How could I ever escape these torturous thoughts?

How could I capture these agonizing memories and send them far away, banishing them to some desolate place so they would never return?

How could I shut my ears to the voice of the demons reminding me of all the evil that I had experienced?

When I thought the very weight of sin would crush me forever and pulverize me into a pile of dust and bones, the scenes playing on the movie screen of my mind shifted to the strip clubs and undercover cops, to the biker bashes and bonfires, to the abuse and exploitation I had experienced at the hands of all the men who I had thought were my boyfriends, and finally to Mr. Earl and the men who gathered in the living room of our suburban Gulf Coast home.

I saw Mr. Earl's fat, smiling face as clear as day, clearly remembering him sitting on the couch in the living room on the opposite side of the door I was staring at. I recalled the details of the first time he came to my grandma's house to pick us up when I was only six years old.

That man was the most evil of them all. As I replayed the scene of that fateful day when we moved out of this home and into the place he rented across the street, I saw the face of Satan himself behind his grinning presentation. Mr. Earl had ruined my life and turned me into a pathetic piece of garbage, worth nothing more than whatever price a man was willing to pay to be alone with me while taking whatever he wanted from my soul.

My mind churned with agonizing questions that left me hopeless: Where could I find freedom from this life of pain and suffering that had me swirling into a hopeless abyss?

How would I ever find the strength to build anything of value?

What use was this wasted, woeful life?

How could I ever make myself into anything but a dirty, drug-addicted harlot?

There was no way of escaping whom I had become, and I felt that if I lived to see another sunrise, I would paint the day as black and hopeless as my suffering soul.

The longer I stayed there, the closer I would come to destroying everything good that existed in that picture-perfect place. The room, bed, pretty lace curtains, and porcelain dolls were not mine; I did not belong in that home.

On top of everything else, I remembered that I had some very serious circumstances waiting for me in the form of several felony warrants. The thought of the enforcement of those warrants caused me to sit straight up in bed, and terror tangibly filled every part of my body. The longer I stayed in the area, the closer I would come to receiving the punishment that the court held in store for me.

Thinking I had nowhere else to go and in my desperation to escape my circumstances in Memphis, I had forgotten that I'd had a good reason for running. Clayton, the place where I thought I would find safety and solace, turned out to be the worst place on the planet I could have chosen.

LIGHTBULB MOMENT

 **The lifestyle of drugs and criminal activity creates a complex web that many trafficking victims find themselves in, which can keep them trapped in stressful, dysfunctional cycles, making them prime targets to be continuously exploited by enterprising traffickers.**

The night was not frilly pillow dreams that smelled like roses after all. Instead, I tossed and turned, tortured by what-ifs and if-onlys. I had a fitful night of little sleep, and as soon as the sun started peeking through the blinds, I crept out into the other room to call my far-away friend Robert to ask for one more favor.

Is This Love?

My generous and faithful friend came through once again, and in record time, my grandpa had me back at the bus station in Jamestown for my departure to Arkansas. I had my freshly washed laundry and all of my worldly possessions stuffed in my backpack that I could sling over my shoulder, but this time I also had a bag that my grandma stocked with snacks and homemade cookies. I also had a little cash that my grandpa slipped to me before he pulled away to head back home to his normal routine in Clayton.

I hoped I hadn't been too much of a burden to the elderly couple when I interrupted their regularly scheduled life. I had tried not to take advantage of their kindness or overstay my welcome. And besides, the stack of warrants that the courts had over my head was sitting somewhere on Detective Devin's desk, so the longer I stayed in town, the closer I was to being behind bars.

Once I had my ticket and found a seat on the big bus, I felt a little safer, but I wouldn't be able to breathe easily until at least a few states were between my legal woes and me. I had to get out of the area as quickly as I could, so I sank in my seat and pulled my hood up over my head, making myself look as unwelcoming and menacing as I possibly could in hopes that I would keep the row of seats to myself for my tour through the heart of the Midwest.

The journey took some time and was not the most pleasant expedition, but all my discomfort and distress melted away once I arrived at my destination, where a real-life knight in shining armor waited to meet me. When Robert walked up to me and I saw the kindness and compassion in his eyes and felt his warm arms wrap around me, I was overwhelmed by a familiar feeling I had forgotten I ever felt before.

This was supposed to be a temporary stop on my way to the next place I thought I would hunker down, but with that hug, something shifted in my soul. Somehow, I knew that I would never go another day without this man in my life. His arms were the only safe place I had ever known, and I never wanted to leave his embrace.

I still haven't left his arms, and over twenty-two years later, we still spend every single day together. Robert became my husband, and he continues to be my very best friend. He has brought me into a life I could have only dreamed of—if ever I dared to dream that I could be loved.

Chapter 14

LOVE WILL FIND A WAY

Can't You See?

25+ years old

In the summer of 2003, I became Robert's bride, and we began to build a life together. We eloped to the seashore and stood by the sparkling bay front in the Gulf Coast town where I had been exploited as a child twenty years earlier. Robert gave me a promise that he would never leave me and he would never send me away. He made me his wife as we declared our commitment to each other beside the water that day. With the vows we exchanged, I was able to leave my broken life behind and join my best friend in building a new story all our own.

Coming Off This Long and Winding Road

Robert was patient and gentle with me, taking the time to show me he was safe. He had the confidence and faith to envision me as a woman redeemed, even when I couldn't see myself that way. He overflowed with the kindness and care that I needed to learn to trust him, when I had never trusted a man in my life.

He helped me find healing and wholeness, and he has held my hand through therapy sessions and wrapped me in his strong arms to chase demons of PTSD back into the dark shadows when the memories of abuse tried to torture me through the night.

As Robert gave me the time and space to heal from the complex trauma I had experienced, he showed me a path I would have never found on my own, and he encouraged me to become the woman I was always called to be. He empowered me to make new, healthy choices. The restoration of my power of choice has been one of the biggest parts of my healing journey.

My husband brought me into his family, and over the past two decades plus, I have had the privilege of celebrating, rejoicing, mourning, and grieving people in a lineage of some of the most incredibly kind, honest, and loving people ever to walk the planet. Robert comes from a respected family, and by adding me to this family line, he has shared that esteem with me as well. I am now a woman redeemed.

Robert unlocked a destiny of love and light in my life that I could not see in my decades of darkness. We now live what would seem like a fantasy if I had glimpsed it as I was being used and abused. Our love story is like a fairy tale come to life. There's a small, ancient book called Hosea[1] that sounds a lot like us. More recently, a woman named Francine Rivers wrote a book called *Redeeming Love*[2] that was made into a movie, and it parallels our story as well.

Learning How to Live

Once I was free from human trafficking, I decided I wanted to be healthy in every area of my life, and that meant making healthy choices every day.

Over the years, one of the major ways my husband has helped me live a whole, vibrant life has been by supporting me in my pursuit of therapy with qualified, licensed psychologists. On occasion, Robert attends my weekly therapy sessions with me, and there have been seasons throughout our marriage when he has seen a therapist to help him navigate the world as the spouse of someone with complex PTSD. We have had some wonderful marriage counselors throughout the decades as well.

Robert encourages me to exercise and care for my body, prioritizing getting outside to walk together every day. If ever a time arises when we don't feel like getting fresh air and physical activity, our German Shepherd, Cosmo, won't let us forget that we need to take a trip around the block to get our wiggles out. We also enjoy hiking in the summertime and hitting the slopes to snowboard and ski in the snowy winters. Camping, swimming, fishing, kayaking, and paddleboarding are other exciting adventures we challenge ourselves with. We always have fun together and spend our adventures laughing at silly inside jokes and holding hands as we explore the world side-by-side.

Not only are these activities good for our bodies and souls, but the quality time we spend together also deepens our relationship. I have lived life at the limits, and after surviving so many extreme circumstances, I tend to be drawn to press the boundaries, but Robert keeps me grounded.

Another way my husband has encouraged me to find wholeness is by sharing his faith and teaching me about Jesus. I'll never forget the day I gave my life to Jesus, on March 18, 2004. That is the day that marks transformation and new life for me, and I have been growing in faith and love ever since. Let this be a word of encouragement to the faith community to continue to make safe, non-judgmental spaces for people like me to find solace and healing.

As a guitar instructor and a former worship leader for a church that we helped build many years ago, my husband is anointed with a musical gift. Every morning, he grabs his guitar, and we sing a song of worship and gratitude to God. Then, we spend time praying for our family, friends, nation, and world and reading Scripture together aloud. This practice connects us with the Lord and sets a positive intention for our day, and we have experienced many years of blessings and joy as a result of our daily practice.

Robert was raised in a faith-filled home and attended a Christian school, and even though our childhoods were very different, the bond of communion we have now has given us a shared frame of reference with which to view the world. I've finally found the invisible God I prayed empty prayers to all those years, and he has provided me with a redemption story. With the love of my Father and my transformation into a child of God, I gained a moral compass, loving accountability, and principles of conviction.

At the beginning of my faith journey, we were members of a tiny, country church that met in the hills on the outskirts of town. That little building with the steeple is where I learned how to study my Bible, pray, and fellowship with other Christians. We sang songs on Sunday mornings and clapped our hands, and the women of the congregation taught me how to be a virtuous wife and a faith-filled believer. My memories of Bible studies, baby showers, and bake sales are formative to the stable, healthy life I live today. I'm grateful to that group of women who accepted and loved me despite the darkness of my sinful past.

As Robert and I have taken this walk of faith together through the years, we have made many more memories of Sunday morning services, Wednesday night Bible studies, small group suppers, prayer meetings, and even all-night worship sessions. The healing, restoration, and freedom I have experienced as a result of my relationship with Jesus can only be described as miraculous. My husband and I have been beyond blessed to make lifelong friends through the church and have grown deep roots in our faith as we have been woven into the global Body of Christ.

On the Outside Looking In

We are far from perfect, and as patient and kind as Robert is, my husband is still human. And I give him a lot to handle. As a result of the prolonged childhood abuse that I experienced and the corresponding years of being in fight-or-flight mode, I have what is referred to as Complex Post Traumatic Stress Disorder or C-PTSD.[3] At times, the symptoms and manifestations of that can be difficult for both of us to navigate.

Even after more than two decades, I still have flashbacks and vivid memories of being abused, raped, and sold. Sometimes bad dreams wake me in a panic, and if another unrelated event triggers the C-PTSD, it can be like starting all over again to find a place of safety and stability.

For example, in 2024, we were in a horrific head-on collision with a truck driven by a man who ran a red light and slammed into us at a high rate of speed. It was a miracle we were able to walk away from the wreck, but the event triggered my brain to overreact to dormant trauma. The bruises on my body faded as we participated in many months of physical therapy, but I am still dealing with residual emotional and psychological damage more than a year later from the activation of the underlying C-PTSD.

Managing C-PTSD has presented a sharp learning curve, and we have had to learn ways to navigate the world despite my psychological challenges. Throughout the years, I have been schooled on healing techniques, holistic protocols, and best practices from a host of brilliant medical and mental health care professionals. I've become keenly aware that it's important to focus on what I can control and to be proactive to set a healthy baseline by maintaining routines that give optimal outcomes.

Some healthy habits I have found beneficial through the years are journaling, maintaining positive friendships that challenge and edify me, and keeping good boundaries. Whenever possible, I eat whole, minimally processed foods, take quality vitamins and supplements, and reduce toxins by choosing natural personal care products. For years, I have been diligent in prioritizing regular physical activity and getting quality sleep.

Studying the physical effects of stress on my body has highlighted the unique challenges I have to contend with as a survivor of complex trauma. My brain and body already have more to process than someone without a history of trauma, so I benefit from anything I can do to reduce inflammation and stress. In my pursuit of addressing the root causes of my symptoms, I am more inclined to choose holistic, natural medicines and pursue integrative and functional styles of healthcare. Others may thrive under a regimen of medicine and therapies managed by a psychologist or physician. Survivors should be empowered to choose our own methods of medical care.

We recently adopted a puppy, "K9 Kanga," and I am training her to be my service animal to assist me as I navigate the symptoms of C-PTSD. Half Belgian Malinois, half German Shepherd, K9 Kanga is a uniquely gifted dog who was bred to serve and was generously gifted to me by her breeder. This brilliant, bouncing bundle of joy has brought an infusion of love to our home, and we know the future is filled with many years of high-energy adventures. You can follow along on her tactical training and development by watching updates on my YouTube channel @survivorsandystorm.

We have been working with Kanga since she was just five weeks old, and I have had revelatory insight into the similarities of how methods and techniques used to condition and train a puppy are mimicked by pedophile predators as they groom and shape the world of a young child. The world I am creating for Kanga is all she will ever know, and she will only learn, grow, and respond according to what I show her, how I teach her, and which actions she is rewarded for. As a tiny little girl, I was trained in a similar style, but I was not in a loving, healthy home, and the results of that grooming and abuse set my life on a destructive course. My opportunity to set K9 Kanga up for success is another act of redemption, empowerment, and reclaiming my freedom.

If you or someone you care about has been through the types of abuse and exploitation I described in this book, you may feel insecure at times or find yourself carrying a burden that seems impossible to bear. Hopefully, some of my suggestions for handling C-PTSD can help you or your loved one discover peace and healing. Let my story fill you with hope that it is possible to find freedom and see recovery despite the pain of the past.

Walking in Forgiveness and Setting Healthy Boundaries

It can be difficult to navigate life after exploitation and maintain a healthy outlook on life. Choosing forgiveness is the only way I have found to relieve the burden and truly live a life of freedom. Because my first traffickers were family members, it seemed easier to forgive the strangers who hurt me than those I knew and trusted. But the only way I was able to unlock the door to personal healing and restoration was by using the key of forgiveness and releasing my anger toward all of my traffickers. My faith reminds me I have been forgiven, and I am called to forgive.

Forgiveness doesn't mean the crime never happened, but it does mean my life is no longer defined by what others did to me. I have learned to forgive but maintain healthy boundaries so dangerous people who want to harm me don't have access to my life. I walk in forgiveness and have wiped the slate clean, but that does not mean I maintain relationships with traffickers. There is no place in my life for someone who exploits others or hurts children.

The road to establishing boundaries is a path each person needs to find individually, but possibly the most important aspect is the support network. Trauma survivors need to build healthy relationships with people who challenge us while holding us accountable, speaking the truth in love.

In my search for healing, I have found those voices of guidance and reason in some of my therapists but especially in the people I interact with on a regular basis. In addition to my husband, I also have some special friendships, including a beautiful mentor who is like a mom to me, and my amazing sisters who each have healthy, beautiful families of their own. These smart, strong women provide healthy and loving relationships and act as my support system.

LIGHTBULB MOMENT

Anyone can start on a new path, in a new direction, and set and reach goals that might have once seemed impossible to attain.

Anyone can make new choices and decide to try new things to get different outcomes.

Anyone can break free from addiction to live a healthy life without bondage to drugs and alcohol.

I may not be the best example of these realities, but I am one example among thousands of survivors who are living healthy, thriving lives today.

You might have read this book with a heavy heart as you realized someone you love—or even yourself—was a victim of human trafficking. Sometimes it takes hearing the truth from an outsider to have a revelation of what happened in a personal situation. That's how I had my lightbulb moment so many years ago. Now I've stepped out of the shadows and I'm living in the light.

I've been free for over twenty years, and I thank God every day for giving me an incredible, new life filled with unbelievable opportunities and His amazing blessings. Gratitude fuels my heart, and I am humbled and honored to be in a position today that allows me to serve others and help shine a light to lead captives out of the darkness.

Makes Me Wonder

In the beginning, every trafficker I ever had looked like a hero. But, eventually, life became desperate and hopeless. The darkness of night was like a protective cloak or a cocoon that insulated me from the ongoing abuse, manipulation, and exploitation.

I didn't get rescued.

Trafficking victims like me often dream of a hero kicking down the door and whisking them away to safety, but the sad reality is that many victims slide down the slippery slope into even more dangerous situations.

Thankfully, I was able to get free and am still living a life of freedom today. Trafficking victims like me are not as rare as you might think. I share my story because it is, unfortunately, all too common. Just as there is a possibility you may have stood in line behind a trafficker at a convenience store or may have a buyer living in your neighborhood, you could have driven right past a trafficking victim on your way to work this morning.

Much of the path I have found to be uncharted, but I hope my story will help others avoid some of the potholes and pitfalls I stumbled through.

Survivors don't all have the same stories of abuse and exploitation, and we don't all share the same journey to freedom and healing. But once they find a way to break free from that situation, survivors can benefit from gaining a higher perspective to heal and live in the light.

I am a lucky woman to have been able to build a beautiful life with Robert, and I count my blessings every day. But I know that ours is not the story for everyone. It's been a long journey, and marriage hasn't always been easy, but it has been worth it. Some days I can hardly believe what a blessed, beautiful life we live.

Where the Streets Have No Name

The hardest part of my experience being trafficked wasn't the physical pain of abuse or the heartbreak of neglect, but the lonely times of hopelessness, wandering through the streets and hotels, wishing I had someone with me who would protect me, lead me, and guide me to safety. No one really *saw me*, and I felt invisible. It was like everyone around me was in an outside world, and no one could ever understand what I had experienced.

This toxic cycle of distrust kept the walls of division up, ultimately keeping me trapped in a world of hopelessness. Because I was an outsider to the rest of the world, I couldn't ask for help. We know there are still countless others wishing, hoping, and praying for a way out of the trap they find themselves in. I want my life to be a beacon, leading others out of the darkness.

Surviving twenty tragic years of trafficking and exploitation was a living nightmare, but now my life feels like a fairy tale, a dream come true.

My greatest desire is that my story instills hope in all who hear it.

A brilliant, successful man named Tony Robbins once said, "Your past does not equal your future."

Did you know that your muscles grow from tearing? Muscle growth only occurs after the fibers in your muscles have been damaged on a microscopic level. What doesn't kill you does indeed make you stronger.

Despite the lies of the traffickers who controlled me with guilt and shame, I was able to break free. The very weapons they tried to use to destroy me are the bricks I'm using to build a beautiful life. If someone as lost and desperate as I was can find hope, you can, too. My story of twenty years of trauma and pain has a *happy ending*.

My motivation is to extend hope to anyone who is struggling to break free from exploitation and abuse.

Freedom and healing are within reach.

Building a new life of wholeness is possible.

Survivors of human trafficking are resilient, resourceful, and driven individuals. We know what it is like to come within inches of death, and that makes life sweeter every day.

Let Your Light Shine Down

Today, I find great pleasure knowing that the things I learned from my traffickers can be taught to law enforcement, equipping those in authority to put traffickers behind bars where they belong. Every time a trafficker is taken off the streets, not only are their current victims set free, but all of the others who were being targeted and groomed have a chance at freedom as well.

I'm honored to train medical and mental health professionals to identify the subtle signs that victims display so they can offer an escape from the tangled traps of their exploitative, dangerous situations.

I'm humbled to train educators to recognize patterns of abuse so they can alert law enforcement and be part of rescuing children like me from being victims of unspeakable crimes within their own homes.

I'm overjoyed to train victim service providers and nonprofits serving in the anti-trafficking space on how to best partner with and serve wounded, broken survivors like me who are just beginning their healing journeys.

I'm encouraged to know that this work is not in vain. Together, we are making a strategic impact in the war to end human trafficking. Because people like *you* are taking time to learn the TRUTH about human trafficking, justice is unfolding, and a bright light is shining on this dark world.

---

[1] Bible Gateway, https://www.biblegateway.com/passage/?search=HOSEA 1&version=NKJV.

[2] Rivers, Francine, https://francinerivers.com/books/novels/redeeming-love/.

[3] "Complex PTSD," Psychology Today, https://www.psychologytoday.com/us/basics/complex-ptsd.

FINDING A HIGHER PERSPECTIVE
Today

When justice is done, it brings joy to the righteous but terror to evildoers.

Proverbs 21:15 (NIV)[1]

After learning the TRUTH about human trafficking, you are likely ready to put what you have learned into action. You saw behind the scenes of my story, and now you know the ways a trafficker might *target, groom, and exploit* his victims. The knowledge you have amassed is a weapon that can destroy the evil practice of human trafficking. Reading this book has provided a lightbulb moment, showing you where trafficking is hidden in plain sight. Now that you have seen the light, you can cut through the hype. The enemy is exposed.

Whether you are a professional who works in law enforcement or the medical field, an educator or provider of services to at-risk populations, or a concerned parent or caregiver of vulnerable people, you can have hope that victims *can* survive and build a healthy new life. You are now equipped to be a part of the solution to ending trafficking.

How to End Human Trafficking

I suggest a three-pronged approach to dismantling the Human Trafficking Triangle, which involves consideration of each side of the equation: supplier (trafficker), demand (buyer), and product (victim).

- Justice must be brought to the criminal traffickers to discourage illicit enterprises from proliferating.
- Education and awareness must be prioritized to inform buyers of how much damage is caused by flooding the market with cash to purchase people.
- We must diligently protect the vulnerable among us. If ever a victim is harmed by the crimes of flesh peddlers or body buyers, it must be our priority to provide an opportunity for healing and restoration for that survivor.

The Strong Arm of Justice

It is crucial to remember that trafficking survivors are victims of a crime. The criminal traffickers and buyers will continue exploiting and abusing more victims until they are held accountable and removed from society, where they won't be able to continue committing their crimes. This is why it is of utmost importance that law enforcement targets criminal traffickers to take them off the streets.

True justice for a trafficker always leaves the community safer and involves every part of the criminal justice system doing its job: a law enforcement agency enforcing the law, a prosecutor stepping in to file appropriate charges, and a judge and/or jury sentencing the offender to a punishment involving prison time, fines, and restitution to the victim. Sometimes, the traffickers and/or buyers may have to register as sex offenders in public databases, which further protects the community from future offenses. Restitution packages can include requiring the offenders to provide recompense for ongoing mental health and other support services the victim may require. Using the monies collected from the transgressors allows survivors more autonomy in choosing their providers and also helps to prevent strain on already-strapped public aid organizations.

As we pursue a safe community built on a foundation of justice, it is critical to support the law enforcement agents, judges, prosecutors, and others within the criminal justice systems around the world who build the cases to put these traffickers and buyers behind bars. These heroes are often overworked, underpaid, and underappreciated, and they may feel like they are carrying the weight of the world. Let's make a difference for these courageous men and women and show our appreciation for all they do to protect our communities.

None of my traffickers were punished for what they did to me. Some of them reached the ends of their lives and died without ever answering for the crimes they committed against me. Others escaped responsibility because I didn't have the confidence to inform law enforcement of their crimes. There is no justice for me or the others they may have exploited. Because of this unfortunate fact, I am motivated every day to see justice and freedom for captives. That's why I have dedicated my life to calling for accountability for those who would enslave another human being.

Still Haven't Found What I'm Looking For

When I was being trafficked, it seemed like a never-ending line of men were willing and waiting for a chance to take advantage of me when I was at my lowest, weakest point. The demand was never-diminishing. To end trafficking, we have to tackle the demand.

One example of a possible solution to ending the demand that drives sex trafficking is found in the Nordic Model.[2] This is a viable answer to combating the vicious cycle that keeps so many stuck in a life of exploitation.

The Nordic Model (also referred to as Sex Buyer Law) establishes harsh penalties for traffickers and sex buyers, partnering with robust support services and resources made available to those being bought and sold. This solution breaks the destructive cycle and crumbles the networks that turn people into products producing a profit.

With the Nordic Model, the money to fund the programs is collected through fines and penalties levied against the criminals who were involved in the transactions. This means the buyers feel the financial sting of their exploitative decisions, and the community does not bear the financial burden of supporting survivors. This model has been successful in reducing trafficking in many communities.

If the Nordic Model is not yet in place within your community, you can advocate with your lawmakers to pass laws with a similar focus. And you can always talk to the people in your life about the harm done to society by participating in the demand for products and services where traffickers exploit people.

Healing Hearts with Compassionate Care

The real injustice when human trafficking occurs is that a person has had his or her humanity taken away. Victims have to be dehumanized to be sold as a product. To maintain a compassionate culture and protect the vulnerable among us, we must have respect for the common dignity of human life. We have to recognize the inherent value each human being holds.

As a society, we can change the dehumanizing reality for those still trapped in the darkness of trafficking. If you are in the medical field and recognize possible signs of trafficking in a patient, you now know the significance of creating a heart connection and the critical importance of providing law enforcement with the information they need to build a case and help the victim get free. Maybe you're providing services to survivors, and now you have a deeper understanding of how crucial it is to allow them to exercise their power of choice, even with what may seem like minor issues.

Building a healthy life is possible, and having the right support system is essential. If you're working with the vulnerable population as a parent, teacher, caregiver, or volunteer, you can take what you've learned about the cracks traffickers try to sneak through and help strengthen the kids you care for to be predator-proofed. You can receive training to become the advocate a child needs to stay safe from exploitation through an organization like Court Appointed Special Advocates (CASA)[3], and you can share the kid-friendly information from the NetSmartz[4] or KidSmartz[5] sites provided by NCMEC. Teachers, public safety professionals, and others serving children can find free courses, in-person training, and programs like Code Adam on NCMEC's website hub at missingkids.org.

As you partner with trafficking victims on their journey to find their pathway to healing, remember that their trafficker stripped away their safety and sense of autonomy. By reinstating their awareness of security and reassuring their inherent value, you will provide the support these resilient survivors need to find true freedom and restoration.

Taking Action: Gathering Resources for Organizations Fighting to End Human Trafficking

Over the past few decades, there has been an explosion of education, awareness, and advocacy concerning the issue of human trafficking. During this time, countless groups have sprung up to offer resources and participate in what I refer to as the "Justice Movement."

Some organizations have raised many millions of dollars for the work they claim fights trafficking, but in reality, those donor dollars funded extravagant salaries for executives, leaving little for programming or survivor support. Other organizations might present a flashy, sensationalized marketing campaign, branding themselves as heroes, while in reality, they are exploiting victims.

It's hard to know who to trust. In recent years, multi-million-dollar anti-trafficking nonprofit founders Tim Ballard and Ashton Kutcher resigned from their leadership positions due to scandals, leaving donors, volunteers, and advocates feeling burned by corruption. Ballard left OUR, the organization he started in 2013, after peddling tickets to a movie supposedly based on his life but admittedly full of inflated claims. Ballard was investigated and exposed for impropriety[6] and accused by several former employees of sexual assault and trafficking.[7] Kutcher stepped down from Thorn, the anti-child exploitation organization he helped launch, after making a statement of public support for a convicted rapist.[8]

LIGHTBULB MOMENT

Not everyone who says they are fighting human trafficking is one of the "good guys."

With the unprecedented influx of charitable organizations in the anti-trafficking arena, it can seem overwhelming to determine how to decide which groups are worthy of partnership and support and which ones may be doing more harm than good. Bad actors who use the cause of fighting human trafficking to promote their selfish agendas are not only detrimental to victims but also do a disservice to all of society.

Reputable nonprofits will often display most or all of these characteristics:

- Operational accountability and transparency, financial transparency, and integrity concerning reported numbers. Nonprofits are responsible for disclosing financial reports annually.
- Survivor inclusion and leadership within the organization's operations, advisory committees, and board of directors. Survivors who hold empowered leadership positions will receive

compensation and won't be patronized, used to validate the organization's "success" stories, or presented as tokens.

- Marketing and fundraising campaigns that include images and stories that are factual and practical, not flashy or sensationalized. The use of imagery containing ropes and chains or the glamorization of the sex industry are red flags that the organization may lack credibility. Claims should be easily validated, and any statistics should be recent and cited from reputable sources.

- Healthy relationships and open communication with other organizations within the same space. Organizations that don't collaborate with others, present themselves as elusive, or claim to be working covertly should be avoided.

When you are researching to determine which nonprofits would be the best soil to sow your family's or business's resources into, a good item to review is the organization's IRS Form 990. This legal document is a public disclosure of a 501(c)3 nonprofit organization's income and expenses for the previous year. Executive salaries, governance practices, program outcomes, and a detailed overview of how donations were allocated will be included in this report, which is required to be filed annually.

Other resources that may give a glimpse into the credibility of a charity include third-party audits and certifications through outside watchdog agencies like Guidestar/Candid, Charity Navigator, Great Nonprofits, and the Better Business Bureau. These independent reports can be found with a simple online search but may require a membership fee to view details.

As you consider this information, seek guidance to decide which organizations you will support. You should feel empowered to inquire of the nonprofit and review its social media footprint with a critical eye.

Ask others in the industry if they have professionally engaged with representatives from the group you are considering, and take into account the information disclosed in annual filings. Reach out to ask for an honest opinion of the nonprofit from people who have a track record of engaging with the organization, whether as employees, volunteers, board members, or service recipients. With a little research, you will be able to confidently partner with the right people to see an end to human trafficking.

Set Me Free (Chains)

Because the truth is finally being told, I believe we are about to witness the rise of a new generation of heroic men and women who are awake to the evils of the sex industry and the damage done by human trafficking. *Men and women just like you.*

These new heroes will be crucial to paving the path toward freedom for victims. Their passion for promoting goodwill will inspire their peers to fight for an end to the exploitation of society's most vulnerable.

You don't need to have high-level law enforcement training, special detective skills, or SWAT Team experience to make a difference and be a part of this fight. For example, my husband, Robert, wanted to use his musical gift to raise awareness about human trafficking, so he wrote and recorded the powerful song, "Set Me Free (Chains)." That song and other songs whose titles and lyrics have been sprinkled through this book are available to download as part of the Lightbulb Moments playlist, which is exclusively available at SurvivorSandyStorm.com/Truth.

Like Robert, we can each use our unique abilities and individual expertise to become involved in the Justice Movement. That's why I host *The Freedom Equation Podcast*—so I can use the talent God gave me as a communicator to spread the truth and inspire others to take action. And if you aren't inspired to compose a song, write a book, or produce a podcast, you can still make a huge impact and be part of the solution to ending human trafficking. Sharing your #LightbulbMoments on social media, rating and reviewing this book online, and subscribing to or recommending episodes of *The Freedom Equation Podcast* are all easy, free ways to be involved.

EPILOGUE: FINDING A HIGHER PERSPECTIVE

Whether you work in law enforcement or intelligence, are a medical or mental health professional, serve as a first responder or member of the military, intersect with at-risk populations in your education or social services career, or volunteer with a nonprofit or the faith community, you can access to training, tools, and resources crafted with your specific needs in mind at SurvivorSandyStorm.com/TheFreedomEquation. And if we are not already connected on LinkedIn, reach out and make a connection at linkedin.com/in/survivorsandystorm.

This fight is hard. It's easy to become depressed or overwhelmed when we see people suffering. It makes sense that we might be plagued with fear when we see children falling prey to predators. But as a survivor, I am calling on each of you to be filled with *hope*. It takes all of us, working together, fighting shoulder-to-shoulder, to eradicate human trafficking.

Every time a trafficker is taken down, we come one step closer to victory, and we are reminded to stay in the fight for justice. When we shift the culture away from the destructive practice of selling vulnerable people, we gain momentum to keep moving forward. And when we hear a story of survival from a victim who has broken free from exploitation, we rejoice and overflow with hope for a new life being built.

Thank God for freedom.

Because you have committed yourself to this journey of learning the TRUTH about human trafficking, you are equipped to take action and are empowered to become part of the solution to ending this crime. You are now shining a light in the darkness, helping others see the path to a world free from trafficking and exploitation.

Shine your light on the TRUTH

and share your #LightbulbMoments on social media!

Tag @SurvivorSandyStorm and #TheTruthAboutHumanTrafficking

*K9 Kanga hopes you'll join us on our journey
to eradicate human trafficking!*

---

[1] Scripture quotations marked (NIV) are taken from the Holy Bible, New International Version, copyright © 1973, 1978, 1984 by International Bible Society. Used by permission of Zondervan. All rights reserved.

[2] Nordic Model Now. "Myth: Prostitution is the Oldest Profession." https://nordicmodelnow.org/.

[3] https://nationalcasagal.org/

[4] https://www.netsmartzkids.org/

[5] https://www.missingkids.org/education/kidsmartz

[6] Herbets, Adam, "FULL DOCUMENTS: Tim Ballard Lied to ex-OUR Employees," Fox 13 Salt Lake City, September 28, 2023, https://www.fox13now.com/news/fox-13-investigates/full-documents-tim-ballard-lied-to-donors-according-to-ex-our-employees.

[7] Gerhke, Robert, "Five Women Have Filed a Lawsuit Accusing OUR's Tim Ballard of Sexual Assault," The Salt Lake Tribune, October 9, 2023, https://www.sltrib.com/news/politics/2023/10/09/breaking-five-women-have-filed/.

[8] Thorn. "An Update from Thorn," September 15, 2023, https://www.thorn.org/blog/an-update-from-thorn/.

ABOUT THE AUTHOR
Meet Survivor Sandy Storm

Sandy Storm survived twenty years as a victim of human traffickers and pedophiles, and she now shares her harrowing story of survival as a weapon to dismantle the evil trafficking industry. Sandy offers a higher perspective, sharing the truth about trafficking as an inspirational, high-energy motivational speaker, podcast host, and author.

Since 2009, Sandy has used her insider knowledge and lived experience to serve the counter-trafficking space as a trusted advisor, coach, and trainer for law enforcement, military, medical, and education professionals, as well as for social service, nonprofit, and faith-based organizations.

Sandy has been married to the love of her life since 2003, and they often can be found adventuring in the Rocky Mountains of Colorado with their best furry friends, Cosmo and Kanga.